FAY

Tyndale
House
Publishers,
Incorporated
Wheaton,
Illinois

ANGUS

NOTE:
*In order to protect the
privacy of many people
mentioned in this book, the
names have been changed.*

Library of Congress
Catalog Card Number
77-083555
ISBN 8423-8213-5, paper
Copyright © 1978
by Tyndale House
Publishers, Incorporated
Wheaton, Illinois.
All rights reserved.
First printing February, 1978
Printed in the
United States of America.

To those who have endured

and

to my parents and grandparents

CONTENTS

Author, Fay Angus.

PREFACE

There is a responsibility in being a product of a now extinct culture. International colonialism in China has bred generations of a people who once shared in its cosmopolitan, sophisticated way of life. Transfused from many separate national identities through the import/export trade and missionary endeavor, the ethos of colonialism dug its roots not only into the soil but into the very lifeblood of the Chinese people.

The culture, history, and politics of China have been well documented through the works of Lin Yutang, Pearl Buck, Theodore White, Emily Hahn, Han Suyin, Edgar Snow, and others. They have left us a literary legacy of a country which for decades has caught the imagination and curiosity of the Western World.

It is a disturbing, yet unavoidable fact that China at last once again belongs to the Chinese; not through the benefit of Western knowledge, wisdom, and influence that for years supervised the industrial development of the sleeping dragon; nor through the implantation of Christian doctrine; but rather through the infamous bloody sweep of the Red Guard and the godless philosophy of Mao Tse-tung.

For the first time in its ancient history (dating back to 2206 B.C.) the *people* of China are being served. The People's Republic of China has at last filled the belly, if not the spirit, of the Chinese people en masse—a major strategic success when one considers that there are currently over 800 million bellies to fill!

But man cannot live on a full belly alone, and the Chinese people, bereft of even their own traditions of faith and expression, will not survive a spiritual starvation. There are seeds of hope under the surface, however. Due to a heavy program of native evangelism and training in the late 1940s, the truth of the gospel endures in China. Our challenge as Western Christians is to pray for those seeds of hope to grow and spread.

This book is deliberately devoid of political analysis. My China experience was that of a child growing into young adulthood. As a child merely gropes for identity and orients himself to the circumstances directly involving his own personal well-being, his vision is simple and unencumbered. It is in this lucid simplicity that I write.

This book recounts a series of extraordinary experiences that have molded my life. It is a story of faith.

Fay Angus
Sierra Madre, Calif.

PART I
CHILD OF
DESTINY

Shanghai

DR. CHEN tested the hypodermic syringe. His fingers probed cautiously around the swollen bruises that merged together in various shades of purple, green, and yellow, all with the telltale pinprick center. I would wake in the middle of the night in a cold sweat dreaming of the thrust of the long needles of the Pasteur treatment!

Cauterization of the wound had not been bad. Nitric acid burned for a moment and then it was all

The Bund, showing the customs house clock and Cathay Hotel dome.

over. A dog bite on the leg, enough to draw blood. Rabies, the dread that roamed the streets of China, met us every day in the form of rats, cats, and dogs. All precautions had to be taken.

Shanghai did not have many strays. It was our suspicion that cat and dog meat (a valuable protein source) somehow found its way into the beef and noodles sold by the street vendors. We never quite knew what lurked in those boiling wares—carried in huge wooden tubs which hung from bamboo poles slung across the coolie's bent shoulders.

To make matters worse, I had an eye for the slightest wag of a feeble tail and an ear for the faintest meow of a lost kitten. This gift, along with the expanding heart of an eleven-year-old, led me to bring home generations of destitute animals. Sometimes we'd keep them and sometimes they'd find their way into the small wicker basket which my mother would take somewhere, and I'd never see them again. It never occurred to me that they were anything other than perfectly all right.

My mother was tenderness itself, and at a very early age she taught me how to feed an abandoned newborn kitten with an eyedropper, use a mild boric solution to wash out infected eyes, and bring half-dead animals back to life. St. Francis, patron of wildlife, was our favorite saint, and I could feel him smiling down at me as I went on missions of rescue under houses, in vacant lots, and in trash heaps. Unfortunately the danger of rabies was always present.

My friend Terry had died of rabies, his body racked by violent spasms, his tongue parched and swollen, his eyes bulging in his effort to gasp air. Hydrophobia, the "fear of water," was as old as the dynasties themselves. The progressive constriction of the throat muscles caused rapid dehydration. This was followed by a slow, inevitable paralysis of the respiratory system.

We had laughed when he got bitten. It was not much more than a nip, and he'd kicked and shouted the dog all the way down the street in sixteen-year-old bravura that made my heart swell with pride and admiration. Five years my senior, he was the hero of our compound. Now he was dead; violently, maniacally dead and buried!

Now my Chinese amah Ah-Nee was taking *me* for my rabies shots. I saw the words "City Health Dept." written horizontally in English and then vertically in Chinese. Swinging doors led through to the hard white table in the examination room.

My hand tightened around the money my mother had given me for a promised trip to the tuck shop to buy a confection after the ordeal. Every day, for fourteen days, I would get a sweet treat at the tuck shop after my shot. This was the eleventh day, I was eleven years old; maybe something good would happen. Ah-Nee always paid attention to numbers and days. The fourth day of the fourth month, or sixth day of the sixth month, always had a meaning—good or bad. Eleven/eleven—would it be good or bad today?

"Here, look, here is the right place for today!" said Dr. Chen, as his fingers found an area low toward my right hip socket.

My stomach muscles contracted as they always

did when I saw the large needle poised for the thrust, and my mouth filled with bile.

"Hiss-s-s, Bapsie, hiss-s-s," Ah-Nee sucked the air in through her teeth to show me how. She steadied my head against the folds of her simple blue gown. *"Hiss-s-s, ai-yah, ai-yah,"* she murmured into my ear.

I screamed as the needle found its mark; then it was all over … until tomorrow, and tomorrow, and one more tomorrow! Eleven down, three to go. I was jubilant; the Pasteur treatment was nearly over.

Dr. Chen gave me a rice-paper-wrapped candy. "You are good girl, Bapsie, good girl," he said with a wide smile.

"Bapsie!" The Chinese could not say "Bubsie." I hated the name anyway. It was a hangover from my Australian grandmother "Janma" Westwood, who called all babies "bubby," and Bubsie I had remained. To the family, to my school chums, through my childhood—I remained "Bubsie"! Fortunately the sisters at the Sacred Heart Convent school held firmly on to "Fay." I could not have stood the nickname from them.

Ah-Nee straightened my dress, combed my curls, and took my face in her long slender fingers. "Eskimo pie or staircase today?"

Ah-Nee was tall and angular with high cheekbones and an air of dignity in her carriage that set her uniquely apart in a generation of dumpy, overfed amahs. Unlike most, she did not wear her hair tightly wound into a bun at the back of her head. Instead she had it cropped short, tucked behind her ears. Her long blue gown emphasized the grace of her straight thin frame and stoical beauty. She

16

came from Shantung Province, in the North, renowned as Confucius' home, and for its handsome men and women, strong coolies, pongee silk, cabbage, and eggs!

Ah-Nee had been married to a bodyguard in the service of a rich Chinese merchant, and her background bespoke culture and gentility. When her husband was shot in the line of his duty, she was forced to provide for herself and her five-year-old daughter Sho-Mao ("little kitten"), whom I only saw on rare occasions. I remember her hiding shyly behind her mother's skirts. The little girl wore huge red butterfly bows poised on either side of her jet black hair that looked designed to launch her off into a never-never land of high fantasy. Sho-Mao fell heir to much of my cast-off clothing, but I resented the fact that she had any claim on Ah-Nee at all. For the mere pittance of $25 a month, Ah-Nee was my own private chattel—I felt I owned her and her time was mine!

I loved my amah with a fierce possessive dependence, and I could be brutally demanding, ordering her to fetch and carry things on the slightest whim of the moment. I was "Young Missy" and she was my servant; any life of her own was totally unthinkable. She was a "day" amah as our servants' quarters were small and had room only for our cook/boy and a wife, if ever he chose to marry. The ideal arrangement was to have a married cook/boy and to use his wife as family amah—a day coolie was then hired to come in and do all the manual chores.

Ah-Nee was not demonstrative and she did not

baby me, but her arms were always around me at the
right times. I think now of how often I buried my
head in the folds of her blue gown, sometimes
staining it with my tears. I still smell the fragrance
of her skin as she clutched me to her and soothed
me with the rhythmic pat on the back which was her
gesture of assurance and comfort. She patted me for
solace, she patted me to sleep when I was ill, and
indeed her pat became an external heartbeat to me.
Occasionally she would tuck a white jasmine flower
behind her ear, and its fragrance lingered in my
room long after she had left for the night.

"Eskimo pie or staircase?"

It was always a toss-up. I chose staircase and my
mouth watered at the thought of the long roll of
sesame-seed-covered treacle to be purchased at the
tuck shop. It lasted forever! Sometimes you held it
high above your head, the end in your mouth, and
started unwinding it upward from your tongue;
other times you bit into the end and unwound it at
arm's length in front of you. Once Asa and I had
unwound the whole thing. We had started, she at
one end and I at the other, giggling and eating
toward each other until we met in the middle,
bumping our foreheads and squishing our noses in
a fighting effort to see who would win the last bite!

The tuck shop had everything good to eat. Jars of
pickled turnips; candy-covered water chestnuts
stacked six-deep on a stick, their bright red glaze
drawing the eye; ling-chiao (horn-shaped seed pods);
watermelon seeds, salted pumpkin seeds, sunflower
seeds, and jars and jars of dried, twisted, or
pickled challenges that I dared not even taste.

Posters of Chinese and American movie stars were plastered on the walls, and at two for fifteen cents one could purchase wallet-sized black-and-white glossy prints of all the current Hollywood celebrities. I added to my collection weekly. Tyrone Power was my favorite, with Alice Faye next. After all, my cousin Ian looked just like Tyrone Power. I was completely in love with Ian and determined to make my eleven-year-old imprint on his twenty-year-old heart and run off and marry him. Little did I know that he would soon be joining up to fight a war, and two years later his grave would be marked by a small white cross on a foreign field—R.A.F. fighter pilot, shot down over Holland.

Not only did the snack shop have glossy pictures of Hollywood stars, but it also had other glossy pictures in another box behind the counter that Terry told me about. Terry had bought them. I never had the gumption to ask to see the box, but I knew about it.

Good old Terry, he had taught me a lot. It was so sad to think of him … Rotten old rabies hadn't killed me, not yet anyway, and only three more injections to go. It looked good. No signs, no symptoms, just a badly bruised tummy. Rotten old dogs!

I loved to hear Ah-Nee tell the story of how she had saved my brother Maurice from a dog bite by thrusting her fist right down the big dog's throat. Or the story of Maurice and the rickshaw: Once he and I had shared one rickshaw coming home from an outing at Jessfield Park, with Ah-Nee in another rickshaw, when suddenly our rickshaw turned sharply down a side street and twisted up a series of

19

alleyways. We banged our feet and screamed, but the coolie went faster and faster while Ah-Nee shouted for her coolie to follow us. Had our coolie seen a policeman? Did he have an expired license on his rickshaw? Or was he running away with us for the white slave traffic or the professional beggar's village? We had heard terrible stories about the beggar's village. Of how they broke and twisted limbs or maimed young children to stir the sympathy or revulsion of the passerby. Fact or fantasy, our school cloakroom buzzed with all the possibilities, most of which were pieced together from fragments of adult conversations around us.

With great presence of mind Maurice had climbed up behind the seat onto the folded hood of the rickshaw, then let his weight drop, pulling down on the hood while his feet dragged along the street. This broke the balance of the coolie, who let go of the rails and ran off while we were turned topsy-turvy. No one was hurt, Ah-Nee and her coolie found us, and we never knew just what had happened. But I have often wondered about the incident and what would have been our sordid destiny had it not been altered by the bravery of one small boy.

The possibility of being sold into prostitution, although unlikely, was real, and the "Door of Hope" mission across the Soochow Creek was well-known among the Christian community for its ministry. It offered a refuge to young girls seeking to escape from sexual bondage, and the hope of a rehabilitated life when they left.

As we walked down Nanking Road, a cluster of

rickshaw coolies met us along the curb, vying with each other for the privilege of taking us to the famous Bund waterfront where my mother worked as an accountant with Butterfield & Swire (known as B & S), the British shipping giant. All of the important businesses were there, the steel and concrete of their headquarters making the Bund skyline one of the most famous in the world. The Cathay Hotel on its prominent corner, the Hong Kong and Shanghai Bank building, Jardine Matheson & Co., P. & O., American President Lines, other shipping and commerce firms from around the world—reflections of the import/export trade which brought foreign dominance in China.

I loved the way Ah-Nee bargained with the rickshaw coolies. She never said a word, just stood coldly by, her sharp eyes darting from one to the other as they auctioned off their own services at rapidly declining rates until the hubbub subsided and Ah-Nee was left with the somewhat disgruntled bottom man. My other amahs each had their own distinctive styles of bargaining, as had my mother, aunts, uncles, Chinese and Westerners alike employing gestures and choice vocabularies. But none educated me to the intricacies of effective street bargaining like the unique reserve of Ah-Nee. She played it completely cool, withdrawing herself from the verbal furor. I liked that and found it an invaluable example in later years when I was to arrange my own rickshaw transportation through Shanghai.

The average rickshaw coolie was spent after eight

years of pulling. The strain on lungs and heart and the engorged veins on bulging leg muscles caused many to die in the prime of their manhood. They paced themselves from the regular steady trot of a short fare (a mile or two) to spurts of speed and the exhausting slow pull of the distance run, which was sometimes as long as nine or ten miles on a single fare.

Coolie labor was the marvel of the Orient. One could stand for hours watching the unloading of freight, or even the movement of heavy baggage on a large passenger vessel. Often this was performed by a single coolie transporting huge steel-and-leather steamer trunks on his back, lever-balanced only by the broad strap that went across his forehead. A wrong movement could jerk his head back and break his neck in an instant; or a miscalculated slant of his body as he trotted forward like an overladen turtle could cause a shift of the mass on his back, make him stumble, and crush him under his load. Most of the jades, ivories, porcelains, teak, silks, and exotic products adorning the living rooms of our Western world were brought here at the price of the twisted, broken backs and bodies of the Chinese coolie.

Poverty was the descant to every song of China. From the little *la-li-tou* (scabies head) urchins who ran along Nanking and Bubbling Well Roads, pulling at the skirts and jacket sleeves of the Westerner, wailing "No momma, no poppa, no whisky soda"; to the sampan villages on Soochow Creek; to the families seeking a night's shelter on the broad window ledges of the Hong Kong & Shanghai

Bank building—it was the staccato of metropolis and country village alike.

In the 1932-to-1941 era, Shanghai had a growing population of over four million. Of this four million, 29,000 were picked up dead off the streets each year, due to starvation, disease, and misfortunes beyond description.

In the midst of this, we sipped our gimlets on the verandas of our clubhouses and steeped ourselves in the sophistication unique to the cosmopolitan gentry of the "Paris of the East."

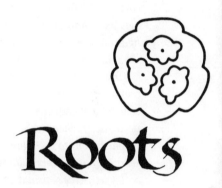

Roots

BOTH MY PARENTS were born in China. I have a valid claim to the yellow water of the Yangtze coursing through my veins. In an era when G. E. "Chinese" Morrison blasted open the doors of that heathen land for the thrust and impact of the gospel of Jesus Christ, my paternal grandparents were sent out by Australia's China Inland Mission and stationed at Kien Ping.

Excerpts from my Uncle Percy Westwood's journal describe life on the mission station:

The China Inland Mission station at Anching.   25

My mother and father were wholly committed to their missionary work. Both spoke Chinese well and passed their third examination in the Chinese written character.

My great friends were my dear amah Wang Ni Ni, the Chinese teacher, Mr. Chen, who came to give the missionaries instructions in Chinese, and especially Yuen Ming, a dear Chinese lad several years older than I was. We used to go for long walks and swim in the river. I spent hours in his small, thatched, earthen-floored house where the food was so much more delicious than ours, and listened to his accurate and hilarious comments on the extraordinary foreigners who inhabited our compound.

Our mission staff was composed of my father who, in addition to running the station, conducted the mission school; a withdrawn elderly Frenchwoman; an aesthetic, redheaded Scotsman (a never-ending source of astonishment to the Chinese); and an eccentric Australian who exercised daily with his dumbbells.

I was fiercely proud of being British. I realize now, however, that all my instincts and preferences were for my Chinese friends and things Chinese. Indeed, my feeling was that my parents and the other missionaries were so busily engaged in winning Chinese souls for Christ that they had little time to spare for the inhibited little boy growing up in their midst.

I felt somehow estranged from my parents and that I had a common bond with my Chinese friends. I fled to them whenever I could. Their soft, padded jackets in winter and cool silk gowns in summer are so much more comfortable than Western garb, and how I still loathe the constricting collars and ties of our dress!

There were moments of horror at the mission

*station—the days when great crowds would gather
outside the North Gate to witness executions. We would
be on our knees in the living room with my father
leading the singing of "Guide me, O thou great
Jehovah, pilgrim through this barren land," my mother
pedaling for dear life at the harmonium organ, to try and
drown out the great shout of "KILL" as the blade
descended on the opium-drugged felons.*

    *But I also remember the great annual boat races on the
river, fairs, processions, and the streets where skilled
tradesmen worked their miracles with jade, silver, and
precious stones. In these streets there was born in me a
lifelong love for the ceramics so perfectly, patiently and
lovingly created ...*

My father (Ernest Westwood) and Percy went to
the famous missionary school at Chefoo, run at
that time by a formidable headmaster and staffed
from Trinity College, Oxford, and Cambridge
Universities, which doubtless explains the excellent
academic reputation it gained over the years. Percy
writes:

*Chefoo itself was a lovely place facing a calm bay and
the distant bluff. Temple Hill, the barracks (I can still
hear the Chinese soldiers chanting along Beach Road),
the low hills at the back of the school with the endless
tinkling procession of mules laden with bean curd, the
lovely temples far above with their atmosphere of ageless
tranquility, and the nonconformist Union Church on
Temple Hill which all the senior pupils attended each
Sunday (except the Anglicans who branched off to
attend their own lovely little church which could have*

27

(Above) My grandmother, "Janma" Hilda Westwood, 1892.

(Below) Janma and her ladies' Bible class, Anching, China, around 1906. Uncle Alan (Percy) is shown in the center wearing his sailor suit and HMS Orient cap. Notice the bound feet on the little girls.

(Above) My grandfather, "Janpa" William Westwood, with Maurice and me. Taken in Brisbane, Australia, where he retired.

(Below) Janpa Westwood with Mr. Muir and students at the CIM Language School, 1906.

been transported from some English village).

My father was a Baptist and my mother Church of England. I asked to be allowed to attend the Church of England (I am moved by outward forms and ritual). However, my father refused and so I had to suffer seemingly interminable sermons at the Union Church!

We had visits from the Royal Navy from the nearby British Naval Station at Wei-hei-wei, the United States Navy, and a German ship that took us to Shanghai for the long winter recess. Occasionally we saw Cossacks in spotless white uniforms—they were attached to the Russian Embassy.

The Chefoo school did not admit Asians. Pupils' parents were mostly British, although we also had the sons of Australians, Canadians, Americans, and Germans. We played cricket, not baseball; soccer, not gridiron football.

I was utterly bewildered and desolated on my arrival at the school. I shared a dormitory with five other boys and often sobbed myself to sleep at night. From time to time our teachers held meetings on the beach, singing lustily, "O happy day, O happy day, when Jesus washed my sins away." They fervently exhorted us to "come to Christ and be saved." Those who accepted the invitation were thereupon baptized beneath the rippling blue waters of the Bay....

One disturbing sentence in this account is: "The Chefoo school did not admit Asians...." Moreover, some missionaries were criticized for preserving their own national life-styles rather than becoming part of the Chinese culture. Yet others went beyond cultural assimilation—they took on Chinese citizenship to further consolidate their commitment to the people they loved.

In the Boxer Rebellion in 1900, hundreds and hundreds of missionaries were hideously tortured and killed. I still wince as I recall reports of their torture and martyrdom. As a child I had nightmares imagining what perils of the faith I might someday be called upon to endure.

When my uncle and my father had been thoroughly grounded in the faith and educated with certification through the Oxford Extension System, they were unleashed to earn their living in the world. Uncle Percy was sent to Canada and eventually found his way back to Australia to join Janma and Janpa Westwood when they retired there. My father Ernest entered the business world in Shanghai, where he eventually met my mother.

My maternal grandfather Ratcliff was in command of a large British garrison in an isolated post in the interior of China, where he trained Chinese army officers. His spirit of adventure had caused him to leave his native England in the late 1800s to go explore the mysteries of Cathay. He and Grandma Ratcliff had some thirteen children, many of whom he delivered himself, and many of whom died in early infancy.

My mother, too, developed a taste for adventure at a very early age and sought out many playmates from the outlying villages of the mountain fort. She tells marvelous stories of a fairytale childhood which my brother and I used to listen to with wonder, begging for "just one more time" on all our favorites.

There was Lin-Chi, the child bride (one of my mother's playmates) who sat sobbing behind her veiled headdress because her husband-to-be was so badly pockmarked from smallpox. This made such an impression on me that throughout my own childhood I took very seriously the Chinese superstition that a girl must eat every grain of rice in her bowl or suffer the consequences of a pockmarked husband—each grain left represented one pock on his face!

She told of the burial of a Chinese Buddhist nun, whose body was seated upright in a large jar for entombment. My mother had her hair braided with red cotton and joined in the funeral procession and the burning of joss paper money and silver *sycee* so that the departed soul would not be without means on the journey to judgment.

The Chinese funeral was a pageant of ritual. In Shanghai, Western influence had contributed "John Brown's Body" and "I'm Going to Hang My Harp on a Weeping Willow Tree" as favorite recessionals, played to the extraordinary harmony of the two-stringed Chinese fiddle and accompanied by cymbals. Professional mourners were hired, clothed in white, to contribute their wailing.

The Chinese believed in three souls—when a person dies, one soul is buried, one remains in the ancestral shrine, and the third goes away for judgment. Paper houses, carts, horses, oxen, and in later years even modern effigies of the motor car were purchased from the temple shops to burn with a fanfare of firecrackers to accompany the soul to judgment. The face of the corpse was often covered

Joss money, burned at all Chinese funerals. The characters say "Bank of the Spiritual World," and specify that the currency could be used either in heaven or in hades.

with a handkerchief so that the evil spirits would not recognize the person.

The use of silver *sycee* was probably the most important ritual. This silver paper money was folded into the shape of a small shoe (this task should be done by women who became vegetarians so that their mouths were clean and sweet to recite the Buddhist scriptures). Joss sticks (incense) had to be burned along with the *sycee* to keep any evil spirits from stealing away the silver money before the soul of the departed could claim it on the other

side. The joss money bank note also had to be
burned for ready cash in death—the currency, good
for either heaven or hell, had a picture of Emperor Yu,
said to be creator of heaven and earth, on one side,
and the name of Yan Lou, emperor of hell on the
other. The whole tradition of the *sycee* and joss
money is said to have originated with the Emperor
Wu-Ti in the Han Dynasty, 200 B.C.

Sometimes furnishings, and on occasion even a
home, would be sold in order to provide for the
elaborate funeral of a loved one. Soothsayers were
consulted (and paid) to choose the correct burial
site and the best day on which to have the funeral.
The countryside outside of Shanghai is covered
with miniature hills, mounds of earth and turf
which are the graves of the departed. The Chinese
leave food on these graves to feed the soul inhabiting
the site, and they assume that we Westerners leave
flowers on our graves so that the departed spirit may
smell them!

My mother would recount for us the joys of
Christmas at the garrison. It was an event planned
for months ahead of time as all the trimmings (save
the tree) had to be ordered through catalogs. Boxes
and boxes would arrive, and on Christmas Eve my
grandparents would spend the entire night setting
up the huge tree, complete with candle lights, with
dolls for the girls tied to its trunk and branches,
and trains and wagons for the boys spread around its
base.

After my grandfather died the family moved to
Shanghai and the children entered various business
pursuits—a few even drifted off to their English

34 *The Chinese believed a devil could not turn corners—the
reasoning behind the construction of this popular
many-cornered bridge over Soochow Creek, leading to the
Willow Pattern Tea House.*

homeland. As I grew up, there was always an abundance of these aunts and uncles around. This compensated for the fact that I knew no one on my father's side (he had only one brother who had settled in Australia).

Once or twice a year everyone would gather for a family banquet at Shanghai's famous restaurant Sun Ya and a whole day would be spent feasting while Chinese parties in adjoining rooms were entertained by sing-song girls, or played "stone, paper, scissors" for drinks, and belched loudly.

Shark's fin soup, 100-year-old eggs that looked like black jelly balls, platters of *bao-tze*, sweet and sour pork, and Peking duck would be consumed, as well as the huge steamed fish, whose eyes were the choice delicacy of the meal. The eyes would be carefully disgorged by chopsticks and handed to the most honored guest, generally my grandmother. In between courses steaming hot towels would be passed around to wipe off not only hands, but faces. (In ancient times this was a means used to transmit smallpox to an enemy.) Finally these courses of gastronomic indulgences came to an end and we were left utterly exhausted and completely immobile for hours.

The personality of each family member was distinctly evidenced by his eating style: the fastidious uncle who would poke around with his chopsticks until he found the choicest morsels; the dieting aunt who took only a spoonful of rice and then swamped it with gravy-sodden savories; the particular cousin who hated vegetables! My manners were Victorian drawing room, but my appetite was

36

strictly street coolie, and I would hold my bowl up to my mouth and scoop in gobs and gobs of rice or noodles with a loud slurping sound that was perfectly acceptable at a Chinese feast.

When the last *"choa-boala"* (I am full) was groaned, family news would be exchanged and the children would go wandering through the maze of that famous restaurant with ears pricked up for the sound of scandal or frivolity coming out of any of the various private dining rooms. The sing-song girls were always the greatest drawing card to our eavesdropping, and we'd press our ears to the thin partitions that separated the various parties and listen to them entertaining the Chinese businessmen. After all this affluence, it was ironic later, during the war, to see these same taipans (big businessmen) working in the kitchens of our concentration camps.

Once we viewed an eating contest held as the result of a gambling game, in which the loser had to eat a *bao-tze* consistent with his losses. These were large buns of steamed dough filled with a variety of savory meat and sometimes sweet beans—very filling and delicious. Rumor later had it that the loser of that particular gambling *bao-tze* contest had died, overstuffed. We had heard that one of the delicacies was monkey brain, eaten directly out of the monkey's skull while it was still warm from the kill. From elephant's trunk to ape's lips, the Chinese offered the most exotic menu in the world.

Food was the essence of life, and a good cook was the prize of a Shanghai household. Families embarking or disembarking would obtain long lists of

My mother, Amy (Mickie) Westwood.

potential household servants, always acquired on the referral system, the baby amah and cook/boy being the positions most in demand.

Even in our own modest home, dinner was at eight and we always had soup, an entree of fish, or breaded brains, or Welsh rarebit, followed by the main course of meat and vegetables, dessert, and generally a bowl of fruit to climax the meal. Finger bowls were part of the day-to-day table setting. Custom was firm, and it was considered an infringement on the "face" of the cook/boy for either my mother or myself to venture near the kitchen—it was his private domain. Once I did peek in and caught him licking the marmalade spoon and then putting it directly into the silverware drawer! With all the germs floating around, one needed cast iron intestines to survive in the Orient!

Until they attained the age of social grace, children had the famous English "high tea" supper and were bedded down early. Whether I attained exceptionally early or was precocious enough to push myself into adult society before my time, I don't know, but I can hardly remember a time when I did not participate in the evening meal.

Scones, finger sandwiches, or just thin-sliced bread with butter and sprinkled sugar would greet me after school for tea (often with friends in to share it) and this assuaged the hunger pangs in the long wait until dinner time.

A few years after my brother Maurice was born, my mother and father took a trip home to Australia to visit Janma and Janpa Westwood, and it was during this sojourn in Brisbane that I was born (in a

kangaroo's pocket, they tell me, which no doubt
accounts for my somewhat jumpy disposition).

My memory of Brisbane is limited to a picture
album of a beautiful coastline and picturesque
gardens with innumerable pictures of Janpa cuddling
me in his arms. He was a tall, handsome man and
I always considered it a shame that I never had the
opportunity of getting to know him.

We returned to Shanghai when I was around
sixteen months old, and after some times of great
happiness and other times clouded by the traumas
of personal difficulties, my mother and father
separated. I was eight years old at the time. My
mother's Roman Catholic faith did not permit
divorce, and she was left with the heartbreak of a
broken marriage and the necessity of earning a living.

She was an intelligent, witty, and beautiful
woman attracting many suitors, among them
handsomely uniformed officers from the many ships
of the British Navy in and out of Shanghai
harbor. The quality of Shanghai nightlife was
unequaled anywhere in the world, and I remember
my mother's metamorphoses from office clothes to
evening taffetas and silks, generally Paris gowns from
Madame Runge's salon. Sometimes she was off for
an evening of dinner and dancing at the French
Club, Ciros, or any other of the high spots in
town. Tuxedo-clad gentlemen, often carrying their
silk hats, would call, and Ah-Nee and I would watch
them drive off into the fascinating night. I fell heir to
the cast-off gowns and would drape them around my
small figure, conducting my own private ball while
Ah-Nee did the ironing.

A Child of the Sacred Heart

WHEN I WAS SIX years old my mother grasped me firmly by the hand and said, "We are going to school."

The Convent of the Sacred Heart, with its worldwide reputation for excellence in academics and the deportment of its students, was a magnificent structure set in several acres of carefully landscaped gardens and walks in the heart of Shanghai's French Concession, Avenue Joffre (named after the famous general).

Our tailor had made me three silk long-sleeved shirts, two pleated navy blue skirts with hem lines a good two inches below the knee, and two ties. In addition we had purchased the regulation navy blue bloomers complete with a pocket low in the left leg (for a handkerchief). Those bloomers were to cause me more demerits than any other factor during my convent days. They were supposed to be worn pulled down low so that the leg elastic clasped just above the knee. But the natural urge was to pull them up to the thigh position where they rightly belonged, and as fast as I would pull them up, Soeur Cecile or the monitor on duty would pull them down for me. It was evident that all daughters of the Sacred Heart were destined to wear red rings from the elastic around their knee tops as symbols of their chastity and modesty.

All three levels of the convent were of highly polished terrazzo and the ornate curved main staircase made of marble looked as though it belonged to a palace in Versailles rather than to a school overrun by the scurrying of hundreds of pairs of blue-stockinged feet. The front parlors (or receiving rooms) were beautifully furnished with potted ferns on pedestals and lush oriental carpets. The furnishings were sparse but elegant, the rooms dark but not dismal, commanding whispers and low monotones in conversations. It would somehow seem out of place to laugh heartily in the parlor, but a muffled giggle was in order.

Reverend Mother Genee, and Mère Alfreda, Maîtress General, met us and the first words I said to them were "How do you do. Are you a boy or a girl?" This comment no doubt entrenched me firmly at the top of their list of students to watch.

The prod of my mother, along with her sweet embarrassed smile, did not diminish my confusion. Their long, swirling black habits with starched white frill framing veiled heads, their silver crosses bearing the flaming "sacred heart" of their order, lying undisturbed on their perfectly flat chests, left me in doubt as to their gender. After all, didn't the priests who served at mass wear long skirts?

We students never did find out what the nuns did with their bosoms, and it was a matter of great conversation and conjecture among us. In later years, as the evidences of our own femininity started protruding through our pongee silk shirts, we would hunch our shoulders in an unsuccessful effort to conceal our bulges. But there they were, and there they grew, much to our embarrassment.

I was not a skirt clinger. From infancy I had been reared under the tradition of the British stiff upper lip. *"Honi soit qui mal y pense,"* was the motto of the Knighthood of the Garter, England's highest order, and loosely translated this means "Shame to him who evil thinks." That, together with "Mind your manners," formed the foundation of my cultural heritage.

My mother kissed me and left me in the care of the Sisters of the Religious of the Sacred Heart. They were devout, committed women "married" to Jesus (as symbolized by the plain gold wedding band they wore on their marriage finger), whose patient, dedicated travail left its pontil, like a glassmaker's trademark, upon my life.

I refused to cry and had little sympathy or respect for those who did. Later, when I was to become a boarder, one of my dearest friends, Ann, became the worst cry-baby of them all and would howl like a banshee each night as she went to bed. Poor Soeur Cecile had to go running for her big sister Frances to tuck her in, night after wailing night. The Compton girls were favorites among the nuns—the elder sister Mary had graduated some years ago, Frances was now in the senior school, and Ann was the newest and smallest moppet to join the student body. The first few nights of her cries for her mother were fun and exciting, bringing just enough zip into an otherwise dull bedtime. But as she carried on for weeks it became more and more of a drag, until Soeur Cecile decided we needed to say the rosary for the girl. It was sound psychology, as most of us would drop off to sleep after the third stanza of "Our Fathers" and "Hail Marys," Ann included!

Our dormitory was divided into many small sleeping cubicles just large enough to hold a bed, nightstand, and chair. If you were fortunate, you got part of a window in your cubicle. The partitions did not go all the way up to the ceiling, so our nighttime fun included throwing notes to each other over the barriers, rapping code signals on the wall, and/or in great daring putting the chair on the bed and peeking over—an unforgivable sin! Our clothes were hung in lockers at the far end of the room and each girl had the privacy of dressing in her own cubicle. It was thoroughly indecent to expose

44

any part of one's anatomy to anyone at any time and we were all unanimous in our opinion that the nuns must indeed shower in their underwear or wash themselves with their eyes closed.

This high sense of modesty ricocheted on me later when I was spending a summer as a boarder in the Holy Ghost Convent in Tsingtao, which was run by the Franciscan sisters. The dorm there was open, which meant we either had to line up for the toilet cubicles in which to change, change under the bedclothes, or find some other covering. I chose to change behind the curtains that draped the windows, little realizing the show I was putting on for the passersby on the street below!

There was an enormous sense of comfort in going to sleep each night with Soeur Cecile, a visible guardian angel, watching over us. The nuns must have switched duties through the night, as Mère Roberta was there to ring the bell to awaken us in the morning. But even as, through the years, Ah-Nee's pat had solaced my body, the watchful care of the Sisters of the Sacred Heart solaced my spirit and eased my fears.

The heart of the convent was the main chapel—the spiritual *sanctum sanctorum* for nuns and students alike. The terrazzo foyer of the main entrance led to massive, carved oak doors through which we entered. The chapel's beauty made it almost a miniature cathedral. Incense from the daily services flowed out and filled our classrooms. It clung to our garments, a savored constant reminder of our spiritual commitment.

A smaller chapel dedicated to the Annunciation

of the Blessed Virgin Mary was on the second floor, and many services of devotion or quiet times of rosary and prayer were held there. Tradition had it that the painting displayed there was a reproduction of a famous mural which, when originally done by a gifted nun, was hideous with shocking pinks and other vivid colors instead of the usual pastels. It was so vibrant that it was draped and forgotten. However, after the passage of several months, someone one day happened to pull off the heavy drape and lo, the colors had subdued and an exquisite work of art was revealed. A miracle? No, just the absorption of paint into plaster. The young Mary, in her obedient response to the call of the angel Gabriel, indeed was remembered by us daily in the recitation of the Magnificat.

The main chapel could easily house 300. The workmanship of the statues, the gold tabernacle, and the ornate altar with cloths embroidered in gold by generations of Sisters of the Sacred Heart brought heaven down to the level of this small child! As we took our personal black veils (white trimmed with lace for special feast days) from their respective boxes in the cloakroom and attended devotions, I could hardly stand the exhilaration of being in so magnificent a place.

The transcendence of God, so often deemphasized in certain practical approaches of Christianity, was here celebrated. I could not understand; I could only enjoy and present my own small insignificant spirit in worship of my Creator. I was a spiritually attuned child—unfortunately, not consistently—but the depth of my being did seek to respond in faith through these experiences. I knew the prayers in my prayer book backward and forward and sought to be approved by kneeling long periods after everyone else was seated during the Ordinary of the Mass.

In the second-floor study hall there was a large picture of Saint Madeleine Sophie, founder of the Order of the Sacred Heart. She was dressed in the black habit of the order and knelt on her *prie-dieu* (praying stool) on a large cloud, with prayerful hands and eyes lifted up to heaven. Hosts of angelic cherubs surrounded her, and she was the daily example to all students. We prayed:

Dear Saint Madeleine Sophie, by the love you had for children and the untiring zeal with which you worked, prayed, and suffered for them while on earth, we beseech you to look down on us. Teach us the spirit of self-sacrifice and fidelity to our duties so that we may be worthy of our name of Children of the Sacred Heart. Help us to keep our souls unsullied by frequently taking Holy Communion so that drawing from this our daily strength we may be faithful to God during this life and one day be gathered around you in heaven....

A recurring fantasy I enjoyed during chapel meditations was that of myself in a similar position to our beloved Saint Madeleine Sophie, and I felt that if I knelt long enough and prayed hard enough God just could not stand for so pure and sweet a child of his to remain any longer in the soiled earth. Surely he would send a cloud to visibly lift me from the pew, and float me right over the altar and up through the ceiling to join him. Somehow I overlooked the fact that the ceiling of the chapel led to the second story, and the ceiling of the second story led to the third story, and I would have to penetrate some four levels in order to break through my earthly bondage.

In my fantasy, all the nuns and students would gasp and prostrate themselves during this celestial rapture and say, "Oh, look how good Fay was. God just couldn't stand for her to be away from him any longer!" They would then feel guilty and sorry for all the mean things they had said to me in the past, or the punishments they had meted out to me, and they would have to go to confession and do their penance. I'd soon be made a patron saint and start working all sorts of miracles. The somewhat shattering contradiction of my vision remained that I was still alive and kneeling in the pew!

On one rather unfortunate day, as I knelt while everyone else was sitting, and trailed off on an umpteenth cloud to heaven, I could not resist temptation. Mère Roberta was sitting demurely in front of me saying her rosary. With all the skill of a proficient Girl Scout, I swiftly knotted the tails of her long black veil to the back rail of the pew so that when the *Agnus Dei* bell rang for the fall forward, her headdress nearly flew off!

The accumulative demerits of that particular escapade moved my desk into the office of the Maîtress General. I had to study under the solemn scrutiny of her chastening eye for one week, and in that time I felt the anger of Almighty God ministered through convent discipline. I was fortunate, I was told, that I had not been expelled!

We were told never to touch the newspaper bundles

48

Children of the Sacred Heart. (I'm circled.)

that frequently appeared on the convent steps. We were never told what was in them, but only that they must be reported immediately. The day I found one, heard a whimpering, and saw a tiny foot thrust from among the newsprint is seared in my memory. I was stunned by the realization that these were abandoned babies—human life thrown away—and I looked around to see if some mother (like Moses' sister) hid around a corner to see what would become of her child.

True to my inbred obedience, I made the report and retired to brood among the overcoats that made the cloakroom a solace to my burdens. Indeed

49

the cloakroom was the alpha and omega of the day student. Here each morning she shed the vestiges of the outside world and entered the cloister of learning; and here each afternoon she prepared to face the family.

On entry to the convent each student was assigned a number (mine was twenty-four) which appeared on her cloakroom hook, locker, clothing, and all her books and belongings. On cold winter days when hooks were overloaded with overcoats, mufflers, and hats it was possible to bury oneself in among them and hide. Mère Roberta made a regular check, but as her mind was often on the business of her daily chores, her check was a hurried one and I never did get caught.

The relationship between the bundles on the doorstep and the flannelette pajamas that we so carefully stitched in sewing class was realized in the orphanage. Each student was permitted to select a name for her "orphan," and she then took on the task of putting together the precut pieces of flannelette as an offering of love for her child. Most of our sewing was done during the annual retreat.

Whether the orphans ever received the names we chose for them remains unanswered, but it gave us all a poignant sense of responsibility and compassion to do the naming. The only trouble was that I was lousy at sewing and hated it with all my heart. I expect to see my little baby greet me in heaven with his body half bare from the badly stitched garments that I so hurriedly and resentfully threw together for him!

The Roman Catholic lessons in silence have served

me well spiritually all my life. Once a year, during the lenten season, we as a student body were called to three days of silence and meditation. The introspection of the soul of an eight-year-old does not take long. So, much of our time was spent reading the lives of the saints, listening to inspiring dialogs or music, and sewing for the orphans. We vied with each other to demonstrate our discipline in not speaking the first word, and even during the hour recess which we were permitted both morning and afternoon, there was a whispered hush among the garden walks as each young daughter of the Lord Jesus sought to maintain her spirituality. We soon learned to communicate through the glance of an eye, or slight gesture, which bred a sensitivity beyond words. It was a holy time never violated. The commonplace pranks were set aside, and for three days in the year I believed God was most pleased with his Children of the Sacred Heart. We learned to listen to the voices of our own hearts and learned how to take pleasure in the quietness of our spirits.

This was the prelude to my first Holy Communion. Its preparation had gone on for weeks—one could not partake unworthily. I confessed every sin I had ever committed and even some I had not committed, so pure a soul did I want to present to my Savior and so clean a temple did I want to offer him.

The examination of our conscience was on three levels—to God, to our neighbors, and to ourselves.

Have I spoken irreverently of God and holy things?
Have I taken his name in vain, or told untruths?

51

Have I carefully avoided all kinds of impurity and faithfully resisted thoughts of infidelity, distrust, and presumption?

Have I disobeyed my superiors, murmured against their commands, or spoken of them contemptuously?

Have I been troubled, peevish, or impatient when told of my faults, and have I not corrected them?

Have I offended anyone by injurious words or actions?

Have I taken pleasure in hearing myself praised, or acted from motives of vanity or human respect?

Have I yielded to intemperance, rage, impatience, or jealousy?

Has my conversation been edifying and moderate or have I been froward, proud, or troublesome to others?

Thus we would accuse ourselves, make our confession, express our contrition, and carry out our penance.

On May 6, just two weeks short of my eighth birthday, I made my first Holy Communion. A state of purity was to be our highest achievement and offering—for how else could one be fit to house the living flesh and blood of our blessed Savior?

Weeks of instruction and preparation had been spent, all our sins had been confessed and then confessed again, and sometimes once again just to be sure. We made a thorough study of the saints and were encouraged to imitate their exemplary lives. I had chosen for my patron Saint Therese, "The Little Flower" of the child Jesus. Her statue stood on one of the landings of the central stairway, and we made our genuflection each time we passed. On the day of *her* first communion she had said:

*I shall always remember my first Communion Day as
one of unclouded happiness. How sweet was the first
embrace of Jesus. It was indeed an embrace of love.*

*I felt that I was loved and I said, "I love Thee and I
give myself to Thee forever." Jesus asked nothing of me
and claimed no sacrifice ... that day our meeting was
more than simple recognition, it was perfect union.*

*We were no longer two, Therese had disappeared like
a drop of water lost in the immensity of the ocean; Jesus
alone remained. He was the Master, the King!*

*My joy became so intense, so deep that it could not be
restrained, tears of happiness welled up and overflowed
... all the joy of Heaven had come down into one heart
and this heart, weak and mortal as it was, could not
contain it without tears.*

I hoped that I, too, could squeeze out a few tears to
show my joy.

Nine of us were to spend the night at the convent,
even though we were day scholars at the time.
Confessions had been heard, and after our penance
there must be no opportunity for sin to enter and soil
the purity of the morning communion. My
mother gave elaborate instructions to Soeur Cecile
on how to comb my curls. The long white organdy
dress over its soft silk underskirt covered me in
symbolic purity. The gossamer white veil was held in
place with a wreath of white roses similar to that
which had graced the head of my beloved Therese. I
held a new white missal and a white rosary with
commemorative silver medals. Nine small brides of
Christ formed their processional down the corridors,
down the marble stairs, and up the center aisle of the

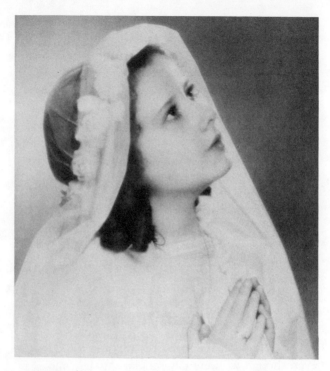

My first Holy Communion, on May 6, just two weeks before my eighth birthday.

incensed chapel to kneel on the white *prie-dieus*. Satin cushions and pure white "lilies of the field" with trailing white bows adorned each *prie-dieu*. We each carried a lit candle which we placed in its special holder on the side of the lily.

Dear sweet Jesus, please help me not to sin in word, thought, or deed.

Dear sweet Jesus, I am so afraid that I will not be pure enough for you to live in me.

Dear sweet Jesus, I am not worthy that thou should

enter under my roof, but please say the word so that my soul shall be cleansed.

Dear sweet Jesus, I have bathed my body, I have bathed my soul with confession and penance, I have brushed my teeth, and I have even scraped my tongue so that the host of your presence would have a clean resting place–please forgive me if I have forgotten anything and left anything undone.

Dear sweet Jesus, please make me one with you, like you made Therese.

My prayers went up from my tear-filled eyes. My recurring chapel fantasy of being wafted into heaven on Saint Madeleine Sophie's cloud was never so vivid.

Dear sweet Jesus, this is the perfect time. Please take me up to be with you; I want to be with you so badly. I don't want these moments to end. I want to go to you in my communion dress, all white and pure and pleasing to you. I know I will sin again if I am left in this wicked earth. Please take me, now....

The service began.

We bless the God of heaven and shall praise him before all things living; because he hath dealt with us according to his mercy.

    The Lord be with you.
    And with thy spirit.
    Let us bless the Lord.
    Thanks be to God.
    May Almighty God, the Father, Son, and Holy Ghost bless you. Amen.

Reluctantly, we acknowledged Mère Alfreda's click to rise, the click to genuflect and turn, and the recessional graced by the beautiful voice of Mère Agnes.

Relatives and friends all joined in the communion breakfast afterward, the communicants still awed by the experience of housing the living host and quietly exchanging holy pictures in commemoration of the occasion: A picture of the head of Christ from Mère Agnes. A picture of the child Jesus administering the host to a little girl: "My darling little girl, always remember this day. Love, Mummy." A picture of the Blessed Virgin Mary with the child Jesus. I had my own pictures to give away, carefully chosen and inscribed, "A souvenir of my First Holy Communion. Fay Westwood." All these I have treasured through the years, either in my missal or in my flat red tin box. Visible mementos of a spiritual love.

The day was too holy to end. I wished it would continue forever. Alas, pictures by the photographer, kisses, and then the dress had to come off, its organdy frills carefully packed in tissue paper with the gossamer veil and wreath of roses.

Divested of my white garments, once again I was a little girl, prone to wander and always doing those things I ought not to have done and leaving undone those things that I ought to have done!

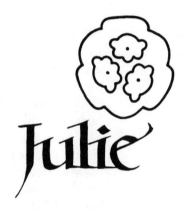

Julie

"STRYCHNINE is the answer," said Julie. If Julie said strychnine was the answer, it was. Julie was always right; she knew everything!

We were walking home from our third viewing of the film *The Wax Museum.* We had sat in the practically empty theater with our legs tucked up under us so that nothing spooky could snatch at them from beneath the seats, and had alternated burying our heads against each other's shoulders with

57

an "I can't bear to look—you tell me when this part is over!"

Now we were out in the street. "That's the second half-starved dog we've passed today," she observed. She lowered her brows and bit hard across the nail on her third finger, a sure symptom of her anger. "We can't take them home, they might even have rabies. We have to destroy them as humanely as we can."

"Hm-m-m," I responded, looking at her out of the corner of my eye.

"Come on, let's hurry." Suddenly she was all action. "We'll get Dad's heart pills—they're full of strychnine—roll them up in a bit of meat, and put the poor beasts out of their misery."

Julie knew exactly what she was doing when it came to animals. I had total and admiring trust in her. After all, she was going to be a veterinarian. Hadn't I helped her shear her angora rabbits—all twenty-three of them—and carefully weigh the soft fur which was to be sold when enough was gathered? Hadn't I helped groom the donkey, Archie, affectionately named after her father's good friend Sir Archibald Clark-Kerr, the British Ambassador? Had we not played midwife to the dozens of kittens which her five cats were continually spawning in closets (and once even under the covers of the bed we shared when I spent the night with her)? There was no doubt, when it came to animals, that Julie knew everything.

We wrapped our weapons of mercy and set about sleuthing for strays. The one we passed on the way home was still there, shivering, crouched against the wall of a boarded-up shop.

"Here, here, poor doggie," we enticed, somewhat gingerly offering our spiked treat of meat. It did not require much encouragement. The hungry animal gulped down the meat in one swallow and pitifully raised its glazed eyes to us for more. Six strychnine pills were wrapped in the bit of meat.

"Are we going to stand and watch him die?" I asked.

"No, stupid, of course not," retorted Julie somewhat impatiently. "It'll take at least twenty minutes for the pills to work and we have only about an hour and a half of daylight left. Come on, let's go find another one."

"Will the pills work just as well on cats?" I asked.

"I don't know," said Julie. "Cats are different in their entire systems, y'know."

"Pity," I said. "There are a lot more stray cats than dogs."

We found one more dog, sitting on his haunches, its gaunt rib cage heaving up and down. He snarled at us as we approached and we had to throw him the wad of meat. One more act of mercy—we lingered a moment and then ambled home. We had two bundles of pill-filled meat left.

"We'll put it in the ice box and take it out with us tomorrow."

"What if the cook decides to use it?" I asked.

"You're right," said Julie. "We'll just take out the pills and save them—the cats can have the meat!"

"Always look out for poor animals," Julie had instructed me. "They can't talk and let you know their feelings. If they're hurt, help them, and if you can't help them, put them out of their misery."

We were completely confident of the success of our good deeds and had every expectation that the poor dogs would keel over and die the instant the pills were absorbed into their digestive systems. Whatever agonizing and convulsive horrors they must have suffered as a consequence of our folly still haunt me.

I had met Julie, who was two years my senior, while I was at the convent. From the moment her dark Italian eyes caught mine, flickered, and then winked mischievously, I knew we were destined to be friends. Her olive complexion and long tawny hair gave her the look of a Raphael madonna. She had the longest hair of anyone I had seen. We were always measuring it.

"Look, look, it's two inches below your waist!"

"Has it reached my seat yet?"

"When do you think it will reach your knees?"

She wore it coiled in braids around her head, but on rare occasions I saw it loose—a shining golden cape. I stood in awe when she washed it. It filled the whole basin. If it should go down the drain, I speculated, would it reach the bend in the pipe?

Julie was my heroine. Wherever she led I would follow, and lead she did, generally into byways that I would never have had the imagination or gumption to dare alone.

Julie's beautiful English mother had died some years back, leaving a heartbroken father with two small girls. Roberto was one of the leading taipans in Shanghai. His estate covered nearly a city block, with winding walks, tennis courts, and lily ponds. It

was furnished in the Chinese style: teakwood
screens inlaid with mother-of-pearl, sandalwood
opium stools, dynasty vases, and silk embroidered
hangings. The elegance prompted us to tiptoe around
the drawing rooms and parlors.

A large black teakwood throne with
dragon's-head arms occupied the place of honor.
"See," Julie would say, "these dragons have a
pearl in their mouths. That is a symbol of the sun
and of royalty." We'd sit in the throne and imagine
what it was like to have been the Dowager Empress.

Cinnabar boxes, intricately carved ivory balls,
within balls, within balls, and a pure red amber
statue of Kuan-yin, the goddess of mercy, all
carefully placed in the best vantage points,
reflected her father's love of the oriental arts. Jade
carvings were everywhere. Jade—best loved stone in
Chinese culture. Legends speak of jade as the petrified
tears of the Imperial Dragon who wept when
northern China was conquered by the Tartars in
the fourth century.

A retinue of household servants lived in
separate quarters behind the detached kitchen
building which was located at the rear of the house.
It was terribly important that Julie and I kowtow to
the cook—who else would make us trays of crisp
fried potato chips on order, or prepare a bowl of hot
chestnuts?

Julie had inherited her father's dark good looks.
Her sister Antonia was fair skinned, blond, and
blue eyed. Antonia was of no consequence to us; she
was a disheveled, overly plump child with constantly
tangled hair who poked her way into our affairs and

secrets. In those days we pushed her aside totally
and without consideration of her feelings. (Antonia
was to grow into an exceptionally beautiful
woman with a talent for sculpture which she was
later to pursue diligently and successfully in Rome.)

It was Julie who told me about the egg!

From my first breath of winter air, I started to
cough—violent seizures of racking bronchitis that
frequently developed into pneumonia. In late
autumn my mother would start giving me massive
doses of Keppler's Cod Liver Oil and Malt (nice)
and Scott's Emulsion (nasty). Sometimes they
helped, but most times they didn't, and I would be out
of commission for weeks at a time.

I'd bend over endless inhalations of Friar's
balsam, my head swathed in towels that stretched as
a makeshift tent to channel the fumes from the
steaming brew into my lungs.

"Breathe deep, as deep as you can," my mother
would say, as she added boiling water to the pot to
keep the steam going.

I'd turn beet red, perspire profusely, and emerge
from the ordeal with every pore in my face wide open
and my winsome curls reduced to soggy, lank locks.
Fortunately, excellence in academics and the
consistent pursuit of my studies from a propped-up
position in bed held me in good stead, and my final
examinations in no way suffered from my seasonal
confinements.

It was after one such long drawn-out illness, when
I shakily returned to the convent cloakroom,
bundled in sweaters, overcoat, muffler, and a tartan
tam o'shanter, that Julie burst into my arms and

screeched, "You won! You won the egg!"

Once a year the sisters held their famous bazaar. Sometimes it was in early spring just prior to the lenten season, but more often it was to end the school year and commemorate the feast of the Sacred Heart in June. At the bazaar there were exhibits selling exquisite needlework, satin-lined and ornately quilted cigar boxes filled with fudge, and best of all, an annual grand prize raffle.

My good fortune met me in late March after a particularly difficult bout with pneumonia. The grand prize was a large, hinged wicker egg that opened and shut. It had been carefully and ingeniously padded and quilted inside and out with white satin scattered with seed pearls. A large blue and pink ruffle of ribbon bordered its horizontal circumference. The egg was balanced on a curved wicker stand which was also carefully wrapped with white satin ribbon.

Julie swept aside my cold, fumbling fingers and unbuttoned my outer garments. "Hurry," she screeched, and grabbing me by the hand she dragged me down the hall to the assembly room. One of her long braids had become unpinned and was flying down her back while her cheeks were flushed with excitement.

A trail of giggling students followed us, with Mère Roberta, monitor of the cloakroom, panting in the rear. On its table of honor stood the work of art. "Open it!" the chattering chorus urged.

Silently, my pale face drained even more with awe and anticipation, I lifted the top half of the beautiful large egg. There inside, lying on a satin pillow and covered by a hand-crocheted quilt of pink, white, and blue, lay the most beautiful baby doll I had ever seen! Her eyes were half open, and as I lifted her out the long-lashed lids blinked wide to show me two soft brown glass eyes.

"Look underneath. Lift the mattress," the chorus shouted.

Julie took the doll from me and I lifted the bedding to find that the sisters had cleverly placed a satin-covered cardboard ledge under the mattress. They had turned the base of the egg into a trunk holding a layette of doll's clothes! Handkerchief linen nightgowns, knitted bonnets, booties, and beribboned lacy jackets. I had won a fairy tale prize!

My legs felt like papier mache and my eyes filled with tears of overwhelming happiness. I looked at Julie, whose own eyes were a brimming reflection of my joy.

"I'll name her Gloria," I whispered, "Gloria, from 'Gloria in Excelsis Dei.' "

"God will like that," Julie said as she hugged me tight. "He will be pleased."

For months I'd dress and undress my new charge and prop her up in her satin cradle, my fingers often fondling each little seed pearl in wonder. That prize was something lovely that touched my life forever. Little did I know that in the traumas that were on the threshold of my destiny, I would spend long hours reflecting on those moments of captured beauty, over and over and over again!

Julie and I went heart to heart through each experience. Our devotion to each other knew no boundaries, and our love expanded with the years.

Tante Sophia and the Dandruff Amah

I NEVER KNEW HER by any other name than "Tante Sophia." It did occur to me on occasion that I should find out her surname, but somehow Asa and I never got around to it. She was my friend Asa's Aunt Sophia and she soon became the goddess of my imagination. I would spend hours contemplating her extraordinary way of life.

Asa had invited me home to tea one day after school. This was always a special treat as Asa lived in the I.C.I. (Imperial Chemical Industries) building in the middle of the French Concession—on a prominent corner of Rue Ferguson, to be exact. The nice thing about a business assignment in the Orient was that the home office nearly always provided housing. Shanghai abounded with compounds for the B.A.T. (British American Tobacco Co.), Jardine Matheson & Co., The Blue Funnel Line, and myriad other international firms. The I.C.I. had forsaken the compound (a cluster of homes around a large center garden or courtyard) in favor of a multistoried apartment complex. This design lent itself to roller skating around the huge perimeter or games of hide-and-seek in its many corridors. Here Asa Merkalova lived, just one floor under Tante Sophia.

"Thursday afternoons and Saturday mornings are the best days to visit Tante Sophia," Asa confided.

"Why?"

"Well, Thursday is the big Mah-Jongg game and the dandruff amah comes, and Saturday morning if we go early enough we'll get some *tzu-fan* and *you-zha-qui.*"

"Let's go Saturday," I said. "I love *you-zha-qui.*"

"No," answered Asa. "Let's go Thursday—you know, for you to first meet her, and then we'll go again Saturday if your mother will let you."

If my mother would let me, indeed! I had no intention of letting my mother find out anything about Tante Sophia, *ever*. Allowing me to be friends with Asa Merkalova would certainly be the extent of her social tolerance.

"The upper deck just don't mix with the lower deck," she'd say. "It isn't that we don't like them; we just don't mix, and that's that!" Colonial class distinction in a nutshell.

"What's a dandruff amah?" I asked. I was familiar with baby amahs, laundry amahs, and a variety of others, but a dandruff amah?

"You'll see," said Asa. "Thursday we'll go."

You could smell Tante Sophia the moment you walked into the apartment. She was the whiff of 4711 eau de cologne that wafted through the smell-combination of scented candles burning in front of her many icons and the garlic and soya sauce emanating from the kitchen. Tante was sitting with her back toward us with three other women, mixing the ivory pieces of Mah-Jongg on a card table. She was a corpulent busty woman with huge hips but an unusually small waist. She was puffing on a cigarette.

"Asinka! Come, come, let me look at you. Who is your friend?"

Asa pushed me forward, and there I stood under the benevolent gaze of Tante Sophia with her placid round face, jet black hair, and strong loving arms.

"Peasant, obviously," my mother would have said. To me she looked beautiful.

"Boy, bring *pirajki* and tea," she shouted.

My appetite jumped at the news of the Russian treat, savory meat-filled *pirajki*. I had only tasted them once before and that was at a celebration of Russian Easter at Asa's.

"Here, sit down. You want to build my wall for me? *Khorosho* [good], you build for me and bring me luck. You, Asa, build for Nadia."

67

My fingers fumbled to imitate Asa's nimble handling of the ivory, while Tante, Nadia, and the others sat back puffing, laughing, and talking in Russian. Once the game started we had to be very quiet—they were gambling and the stakes were high.

North Wind, South Wind, East Wind, West Wind—Bamboo (Tiao), Dots (Tung), Characters (Wan)—Red Dragon, Green Dragon, White Dragon—Chow, Pung, and the magnificent razzle (mixing of the pieces) at the end of a hand! I had entered a new world.

Tante Sophia was in a jolly mood, so she must have done well. After the game she let us put the ivories away in their beautiful carved teak box.

The dandruff amah had arrived. We had watched her slip quietly into the room—so as not to disturb the play—and set out her combs, cottons, and lotions. She was waiting and ready when the game was over.

Tante waved her guests out, "*Khorosho, khorosho* [good, good]." She settled herself in one of the host chairs from the dining room. The amah placed a blue cloth around her shoulders, wadded up a towel at the nape of her neck, and proceeded to place cotton wool up through the fine teeth of her comb. The cotton could later be pulled through to clean the comb of all the accumulated dirt and dandruff. Part and scratch, part and scratch, the scraping rhythm systematically went through Tante's fine hair.

Tante Sophia's huge bulk seemed to visibly grow and spread over and out through the sides of the heavy chair as she sank deeper and deeper into comfort, her eyes shut, a forgotten cigarette which had by now gone out still dangling from her lips.

Part, scratch, part, scratch—the flakes of dandruff snowed down onto the blue cloth, and the cotton wadded up in the teeth of the comb got dirtier and dirtier. From time to time the amah would take the blue shoulder cloth and proudly show it to Tante to gain approval for all the fallen dandruff, shake the cloth out a window, and start again.... Wisps of hair stood up all over Tante's head.

"How long will she do it?" I whispered to Asa.

"Sshush," hissed Asa. "Don't let her remember we're still here!"

When she was done, the amah sprinkled lotion through the scalp and then massaged it gently, running her fingers through and through the wild disarray. A final combing to order and the procedure was completed—Tante Sophia was sound asleep.

For weeks afterward I'd part and scratch my head, sadly only shaking loose a few flakes of dandruff here and there. I stood in awe of Tante Sophia; never had I seen anyone with so much dandruff!

I could hardly wait until the following Saturday.

"Mummy, can I go and play with Asa today?"

"What are you two going to do?"

"We'll probably spend most of the morning skating and I'll be home for lunch."

Not only would I see Tante again, I'd get to meet her husband. I trembled at the thought. Would he be fierce, gentle, angry, kind? Was he Russian, English, Chinese?

He was English—a huge man, 6′2″ at least, and how he adored his wife. Indulgent to a fault, he'd call her endearments and kiss her often publicly. When we arrived they were both still in bed.

"Ha, Asinka, come in, come in," she yelled from the bedroom. "We're eating here."

Since they were childless, they were always overjoyed to see their little Asa. We both climbed onto the bed and joined in the feast of *tzu-fan* and *you-zha-qui*.

Of all the street food, *you-zha-qui* was my favorite. It consisted of long strips of twisted dough deep-fried in peanut oil. The *you-zha-qui* vendors carried their steaming barrels, balanced on bamboo poles, as they passed through the streets hawking their wares, Some also sold noodles in chicken broth, or hot chestnuts.

It was one of my greatest delights to run around stuffing myself with as many of these delicacies as I could afford, my money never appeasing my appetite, which made my mother wonder why on earth I had no desire for the formal European dinners served so elegantly at our house each evening!

The *tsi-ven* was a sweet, sticky rice ball stuffed with a *you-zha-qui* in its center. The vendor would use a steaming cloth to form the rice ball (frequently using the same steaming cloth to wipe his brow). Then he'd poke his fingers through it to make the opening for the *you-zha-qui*. To me it was the most delicious treat of all. It was commonly eaten by the Chinese for breakfast; it was commonly eaten by me anytime!

70

After our visit we went and sat on the garden wall to put on our roller skates, and I discovered from Asa that Tante Sophia had divorced one husband, the second had died, and this one was number three. This third husband seemed very happy with Tante in spite of her slovenly ways and appearance. Asa told me that at one time she had been a prominent Russian opera singer; she never sang now, and she chain-smoked cigarettes. She rarely went out, but on the few occasions when she did she would dress up in her fox stole and fur hat, and it was easy to imagine her creating a stir in any opera house.

Tante Sophia was very generous and always had good things for us when we'd come over. We loved her with awesome curiosity and visited her as often as we could.

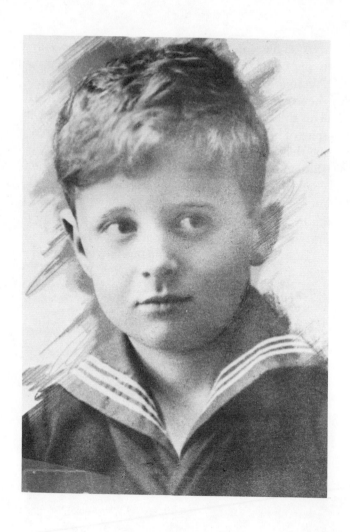

My brother Maurice.

Tsingtao

TSINGTAO was tiger lilies growing on cliffs and
donkey races in huge straw coolie hats. Tsingtao was
the percussion of wind and waves with fast moving
clouds hurling animal shapes across the sky. Most of
all, Tsingtao was pounding surf tracing patterns of
seaweed in the sand and the staccato of pebbles
being sucked back to sea at high tide. Tsingtao was
the pivot of our summer holidays and the utopia in
which my imagination thrived.

73

Developed by the Germans in 1898 and then held by the Japanese from 1914 to 1922, the city boasted reflections from both cultures. Industry thrived and the University of Shantung lent an academic quality to the community. Tsingtao's beautiful rocky promenades and cooling sea breezes made it a popular summer resort. It caught the exodus from the steaming cities during July and August and whipped new life into drenched spirits.

From the time I was eight I was sent up to Tsingtao in care of the captain on one of the Blue Funnel Line steamers. My mother knew all the captains on the China fleet and I was introduced to them summer by summer as I went to spend my vacation with the sisters of the Holy Ghost Convent.

As the only little girl traveling alone, I soon became the darling of the cruise and learned to manipulate my position to the best advantage. I sat at the captain's table, had the total run of the ship, and was frequently escorted by one of the officers to observe navigation on the bridge.

I learned the stars by name and had a sip of most of the cocktails proffered from the bar. With a toss of my curls and a winsome smile I could finagle a plate of dessert from the steward between meals, and if I wasn't getting enough attention I could always squeeze out a tear, pout, and whimper, "I miss my momma!"

The truth was, I didn't miss my momma at all and I was totally in my glory for the short trip up the China coast. I would spend the first month of summer holidays with the nuns, and then my mother

We took annual trips to Tsingtao on the famous Blue Funnel Line.

would bring my brother up and we'd all rent a cottage together for the remainder of the season.

In direct contrast to the somber black habits of the sisters of the Sacred Heart, the nuns of the Holy Ghost Convent wore white from veil to shoe. They were a nursing order, and how they happened to found a small teaching convent in the heart of Tsingtao I really don't know.

The summer atmosphere was one of recreation with moderate attention to studies for a couple of hours a day. We took innumerable walks up

mountain paths, and, of course, spent endless
hours frolicking on the beach while Mère Anna
Marie sat on a small camp stool under a large black
umbrella. Her sharp spectacled eyes darted among us
to keep a constant count. On occasion she would
rush to the water's edge screaming in her thick
German accent, "Bapsy, Bapsy, you haf gone too
far."

She looked like a large flapping white seagull,
and it seemed that through all the wet sand and
dripping children she never soiled her white
habit—an absolute miracle, I was convinced.

She marched us in long straight lines up and
down the beach promenades and everyone would
stop, smile, and stare at the convent girls taking
their outing. I would frequently break ranks to
clamber up the rocky cliffs for a wild flower or one of
the beautiful orange spotted tiger lilies that were my
favorites, only to be severely reprimanded.

"Bapsy, dat flower is for efferyone, not jus for
you! Now, look vot you haf done! Dat cliff has no
flower now!"

Nevertheless, "dat flower" which "vos for
efferyone" was pressed carefully to add to my summer
collection of leaves and seashells, which was boxed in
tissue paper and taken out through the winter
months for a moment's savored memory.

During meal times we were permitted to speak
only French. It was obvious that the sisters of the
Holy Ghost Convent were not a cooking
order—the food was ghastly and that, combined
with our limited French vocabulary, made meals a
frustrating experience for us. If we were too silent,

Mère Gabrielle would read to us—in French. We took turns in trying to keep up the fractured conversation and choked down the boiled vegetables and steamed puddings as rapidly as we could.

One day during lunch, while we were listening to an umpteenth reading of the poem *La Cigale et La Fourmi,* Mère Gabrielle hurried into the dining hall and, after whispering a few words to the sister on duty, took me gently by the hand and said, "Fay, you are excused. Come with me, please."

We went into one of the cozy corners in the large recreation room adjoining the dining hall. These were bay windowed alcoves across which a curtain could be drawn to make a private niche for conversation, counsel, or private reading. While she was drawing the drapes I heard the muffled scurrying of feet down the hall to the chapel.

Mère Gabrielle sat down and drew me to her, putting one hand tenderly on my head. Her pale French beauty had started to fade and crows' feet crinkled the edges of her soft blue eyes.

"*Ma chère petite* Fay, your brother Maurice has gone to be with Jesus."

My brother Maurice, of the laughing eyes and rickshaw rescue?

"He is with Jesus, little Fay," she whispered. As she steadied my sobbing head against her shoulder she told me of the burst appendix, the surgery, and the peritonitis.

"Come now, we must go to the chapel. The others are waiting there for us. We will say the rosary for him and pray for your dear mother."

She placed my black chapel veil over my head
and, taking my small cold hand in hers, led me to
the chapel.

"Hail Mary, mother of God. Blessed art thou
among women..."

Maurice, who only last month had shaved all the
hair off the teddy bear that lay on my bed upstairs. I
wanted to rush to that teddy bear and fling him
against the wall! But convent girls are
self-controlled and we had to kneel in the chapel
and say the rosary.

"... and blessed is the fruit of thy womb, Jesus."

Maurice, who had taught me how to hold my
breath and dive through the huge breakers! Who put
sand crabs down my bathing suit and caterpillars in
my pajama pockets! Maurice, who dared me to
swim out to the raft, throwing me his inner tube,
which I missed, and then getting us stranded out
there drifting into deeper water until Mother had to
rush in, clothes and all, to rescue us!

"Holy Mary, mother of God, pray for us sinners
now and *at the hour of our death*, Amen."

Where were you, holy Mary, mother of God, at
the hour of my brother's death?

I had grown up with death. It was strewn
around the streets of Shanghai in all shapes and
sizes. Flood season always left behind an epidemic of
cholera. The huge trucks would roll up and down the
streets picking up the bodies—dehydrated corpses
with black gaping mouths and rolled back eyes.

I knew the smell of death and had watched the
maggots eat into the decaying flesh of a dead
sparrow. I had seen death stripped as naked as the

78

newspaper-wrapped abandoned babies; and death dressed up, like the elderly sister of the Sacred Heart, propped up in her bed with her rosary entwined around her hands—so pale and beautiful that she looked like a fragile angel. We students made our genuflection and bade her good-bye.

But I had not before experienced the personal *loss* of death. At nine years old I was introduced to grief. With downcast eyes, stifling back the sobs, I followed Mère Gabrielle out of the chapel.

"Would you like some time alone, Fay? A quiet time? Or would you like to be with me for a while?"

"Alone, please, by myself."

"In the cozy corner?"

"No, please, may I go to the grotto of the Virgin Mary?"

In a corner of the garden, the grotto caught the sorrow of my confused heart. Benevolent Mary, with her hands folded in prayer, looked down at me with painted eyes.

"I don't want him with Jesus ... I want him here with ME!"

I rubbed my thumb and forefinger along the rough edge of the granite stones that formed the grotto and took peculiar pleasure in the stinging pain.

"I want him to dare me to jump from the sixth step down ... I want him to operate on my dolls ... most of all I want him to give me a push and send me flying across the lawn, or to pull my hair, or to tease me, running around the dining room table with a beetle in his hands! I want him anywhere, but not up there, dead, with Jesus!"

My fingers bled and I sucked them. There I knelt,

a hunched-over, broken figure at the feet of the statue of Mary.

My mother came to Tsingtao to take me home. We took long walks, arm in arm along the beach. Malignant sadness lined her face, and as we sat on the rocks, looking out to sea, constant tears rolled slowly down her cheeks.

Intermission

THE FIRST TIME I saw Audrey King she was
perched high on the stage rafters of the Lyceum
Theatre, portraying the golden cock in the ballet
"*Coq d'Or.*" Her shimmering costume, her
plume-encrusted helmet, and the ferocity of her
sharp eye movements as she turned her head to the
audience before her breathtaking leap down to the
stage quickened my pulse. Suddenly I was introduced
to a world in which I knew I belonged! From

81

thenceforth, music to me meant movement—it was to be seen as well as heard.

With the help of Nicholai Svetlanoff and other brilliant dancers who had fled Russia as a result of the revolution, Shanghai had formed a ballet company in the grand traditions of Petipa. *The Sleeping Beauty, Swan Lake,* and the beloved *Nutcracker Suite* made Tchaikovsky my favorite composer, and for hours on end I was no longer just Fay, small student of the Sacred Heart. Suddenly, transformed by a chiffon scarf or two, I was Princess Aurora, or Odette/Odile, and most of all I was the Sugar Plum Fairy! I spun and twirled and tried to stand on my bare toes.

My mother enrolled me in Audrey King's Studio of the Dance where, from the time I was five years old, I was taught to examine and discipline the rhythms of my body. The King studio was based on the principles taught by the Royal Academy's London school. A slow, simple method of classroom techniques were used. These were demonstrated for parents and friends on special "open studio" occasions. In contrast, the Sokolsky school staged lavish productions performed in full ornate costumes, with techniques based on the Russian methods. Several of my friends attended this school, and how I envied their frilly appearances with heavily painted faces several times a year.

From the wobbly *pliés* (bending the knees with the back held straight) of the baby classes to the precise *fouettés en pointe* (whipping movements of the raised leg) of the professional students, Audrey King demanded attention and serious, determined effort. A recital in simple form was given at the Lyceum once a year. All our relatives turned out en masse to see my debut at age six, dressed in a pink party frock, rain boots, and umbrella for the raindrop ballet. A picture of me and three other little girls, sweetly posed, appeared in the *North China Daily News,* which early notoriety made me flounce my head and feel superior among my peers.

Indeed, it did not take me long to discover that I liked center stage, and especially the spotlight. Our *pliés, pointe tendu,* and *grande battements* (large kicks) were done to the music of Chopin, Offenbach, Debussy, Rimsky-Korsakov, and of course my beloved Tchaikovsky. We waltzed and held our shaky arabesques with Strauss, and there are familiar passages in all the great symphonies that I find difficult to dissociate from our exercises at the *barre.* The dance enriched my music appreciation.

Unfortunately my music appreciation did not enrich the dance! A "well-rounded" education, embracing all the arts, is the heritage of all young ladies of good breeding. My mother enrolled me in private piano lessons with Madame Papov, who taught at the convent twice a week by special arrangement with the sisters.

Five music cubicles, each holding their upright Steinway, comprised the Music Department at the Sacred Heart. We were required to practice for half an hour daily, and the banging and the thumping that came from the cubicles during these sessions must have been accepted partially as flagellation to the spirits of the patient, long-suffering nuns. We stomped on the "loud" pedal and tried to outdo each other in crescendo.

Madame Papov was a diminutive woman with thin lips. If we played an incorrect note, we would feel the sting of the rap of her ruler. I sat on the piano bench in a state of hate each dreaded week.

"Nyet," she would say, "again...." and again, and again!

Father O'Flanagan, concealed in his confessional booth the following day, must have grinned as he heard the familiar "forgive me, I have sinned in thought..." from all the music students.

At last my mother accepted the fact that I had no talent for the piano. We moved on to the violin, and three sessions later I was free! My feet continued to tap and my body continued to sway, and there was no doubt that movement was meant to be my mode of expression.

I strained my muscles and stretched my ligaments to perfect the difficult steps of ballet. The goal for the junior student was the final grand promotion to *pointe* (toe) shoes! After years of *echappes, releves,* and *changements,* her muscles at age twelve should be developed sufficiently to go on toe. I could hardly wait.

We had just completed our annual recital—"Who Killed Cock Robin?"—in which I had my first solo part, the hawk policeman. The ingenuity of the wardrobe committee had produced a costume of yellow tights dyed in curry powder (they left me with jaundiced legs for several weeks).

The toe shoes came, and I found that with them came, rather than the exhilaration of exhibiting the beautiful "line" they permitted, aching feet and blisters. We soaked our feet in salt water, darned the tips of our satin *pointe* shoes (to make them last longer and keep from skidding), and put bits of lamb's wool over our toes for protection, but the blisters still came. I learned, however, that discomfort is no excuse and one must "continue..." Continue to strive, continue to improve, and continue to master. A credo I was to apply throughout my life.

From the opening *plié* of class to the final *reverence* (stage bow to the teacher) I was in ecstasy. I danced whenever I could and choreographed my own adagios with the larkspurs in the garden. In later years I was to interpret the jungle drum beat which stirred my primitive instincts, and to defy gravity in the arms of a partner in *pas de deux*. The disciplines of a professional dancer bend so much of the imagination to the necessities of technique, but I was a child, and I saw dance movement in everything from the quivering of the silver birch leaves, to the tipping wings of a flight of birds, to the parade of a stream of ants in the crack of a sidewalk.

There are expressions that can only be met through the whirling abandonment of the body—David demonstrated this when he "danced before the Lord." The exuberance of rhythm.

It was an era of romantic movies. Jeanette MacDonald and Nelson Eddy, Ginger Rogers and Fred Astaire sang and danced their way through musicals. Practically every major film had its ballroom scene with swirling skirts and uniforms embellishing the dance of courtship.

I watched my mother in her taffeta and chiffon evening gowns slip out to dance the night away at the French Club and yearned for the arms of a strong man to crush me in a passionate tango or twirl me in a lighthearted waltz. I was growing up.

Betty Dorset lived in one of the taipan houses. It was a stately mansion with rolling green lawns, and, best of all, a large glassed-in conservatory furnished in comfortable white wicker. Potted ferns and philodendron made an excellent camouflage from prying eyes. The main attraction of Betty to me was meeting her two brothers and their various cousins and friends. I'd try my hardest to wiggle my way into an invitation to tea after school, as this meant a wind-up gramophone, records of most of the big bands of the forties, and an opportunity to practice the fox-trot with whoever was on hand. In a pinch we girls would dance together. This was quite chaotic as none of us cared to "lead," and we generally ended up quarreling our way through a perfectly good afternoon.

That's where I met Keith. Sixteen going on seventeen, he was the answer to a young maiden's prayer. Slender and tall with carefully groomed blond hair and dark brown eyes, he had the polish and *savoir-faire* that came from mixing with embassy circles throughout his young life. And could he dance!

My lithe body and adroit footwork made me a favorite partner despite the disparity in our ages, and he soon taught me all the variations to the quick step. The rumba and the tango came next. He did not have to teach me how to waltz—I already knew and was able to teach him a few embellished turns that I had picked up from the ballet studio. He showed up more and more frequently, and we danced together for hours, much to the chagrin of the other girls and the annoyance of other boys who wanted me to teach them a few tricky steps. Occasionally the others would leave in disgust to whack out a game of tennis on the courts that were part of the estate.

These were especially glorious occasions as I then had Keith all to myself. Before long we'd dance ourselves out and then collapse in a breathless panting heap on the chintz-covered sofa. I was in his arms and soon found out that he could kiss as well as he could dance—perhaps even better! I also found out that I liked kissing as much as I liked dancing—perhaps even more so! It became a somewhat frustrating decision as to when to stop dancing and when to start kissing. We soon became referred to as "those two" and were left pretty much alone.

Julie was of course my close confidante, and we analyzed together our growing emotional dimensions. Her father had become deeply involved with a beautiful young Eurasian girl, which prodded us to even further curiosities about sensual possibilities. The cloakroom conversation buzzed with smutty distortions and Mère Roberta must have wondered about the sudden clipped silence when she entered the room.

The chastity of my body and purity of my mind and spirit were being marginally challenged. The growing urges of adolescence were in direct conflict with the strict morality of convent upbringing.

"Your guardian angel sees everything you do," whispered Julie.

"Does she know everything I think, too?" I trembled.

"I don't think so," replied Julie. "I think only God knows that." God knowing that was bad enough.

"Do you suppose my brother Maurice, or someone we know who's dead could be my guardian angel?"

"No, definitely not. Angels are created angels and people are created people," Julie emphasized.

"How do you know?"

"I asked Monseigneur when my mother died. I thought maybe she would become an angel." A sad and wistful look had come into Julie's eyes and I knew the conversation was over.

The protective assurance of a guardian angel was one thing. Had we not repeated over and over, "Angel of God, my guardian dear, to whom his love commits me here. Ever this day be at my side, to light and guard, to rule and guide"? But the prying eyes of a guardian angel was another. I wished somehow that Julie had not told me that.

Just how I would have weighed in on the balances of moral judgment was left undetermined, as the guns of war were steaming across the Yellow Sea and would soon blast open the lives of natives and aliens alike, congested in all the large cities of the Far East.

PART II

P · O · W

14/14

公園前収尸

SPEED LIMIT 15 MILES PER HR

(Above) Taken during the 1937 Japanese/Chinese conflict. The characters say to "collect the corpses in front of the park."
(Below) Caged death. In this punishment offenders were strung up in cages and left to die.

Bridge House

THE ANTHEM OF WAR is the cry of the wounded, and its forage the blood of the innocent. Japanese invasion was nothing new in China. In 1894 the battle was over Korea. In 1937, in the famous Marco Polo Bridge incident outside of Peking, the Japanese had breached the Great Wall, and their soldiers soon swarmed over Northern China. In Shanghai a major battle erupted, bringing furious resistance by Generalissimo Chiang Kai-shek's army.

It was calculated that some 450,000 Chinese died in the conflict within a three-month period. The British evacuated their nationals.

At the time, we were on a ship due to return to Shanghai from an annual summer holiday at Tsingtao. The ship was diverted to Hong Kong, where we rode out the period of conflict in crowded quarters at Repulse Bay.

The 1937 fight spread a wake of atrocities over the villages and cities of China, impacting in blood the mutual hatred of the Chinese and Japanese. With a large population of Japanese entrenched in the Yantzepoo district of Shanghai, across the Soochow Creek from the International Settlement, the city was well primed for the explosion of the Pacific War in December 1941.

In the early hours of Monday, December 8, a Japanese destroyer steamed down the Whangpoo River and sank the 310-ton British gunboat *Peterel* (all hands were lost). Explosions, fire, and billows of black smoke threw the Bund waterfront into sudden panic; the destroyer proceeded downstream and captured the United States gunboat *Wake.*

The Japanese invasion had started, and within a few short hours occupation forces marched into the city. Shanghai was under capture, having no resistance to offer. The United States Marines had been pulled out only a week before, and all British Army units had been withdrawn earlier during heavy European conflict.

The Pacific was at war, under declaration by Hirohito, whose text of proclamation appeared in the *New York Times,* Monday, December 8, 1941:

We, by the grace of Heaven, Emperor of Japan and seated on the throne of a line unbroken for ages eternal, enjoin upon thee, our loyal and brave subjects. We hereby declare war upon the United States of America and the British Empire....

It has been truly unavoidable and far from our wishes that our Empire has now been brought to crossed swords with America and Britain. More than four years have passed since China, failing to comprehend the true intentions of our Empire, and recklessly causing trouble, disturbed the peace of East Asia and compelled our Empire to take up arms.

Although there has been reestablished the National Government of China, with which Japan has effected neighborly intercourse and cooperation, the regime that has survived at Chungking, relying upon American and British protection, continues its opposition.

Eager for the realization of their ambitions to dominate the Orient, both America and Britain, by supporting the Chungking regime, have aggravated disturbances in East Asia. Moreover, these two powers, inducing other countries to follow suit, increased military preparations on all sides of our Empire to challenge us. They have obstructed by every means our peaceful commerce and finally resorted to a direct severance of economic relations menacing gravely the existence of our Empire....

We rely upon the loyalty and courage of our subjects in our confident expectation that the task bequeathed by our forefathers will be carried forward and that the sources of evil will be speedily eradicated and an enduring peace established in East Asia, preserving thereby the glory of our Empire.

The era of *kamikaze* began. Japanese planes flew over the International Settlement of Shanghai dropping leaflets stating that the city had been captured and telling people to remain calm and to go about their business as usual. By nightfall barbed-wire barricades had been thrown up, sectioning off the city. Curfews were set, and within a few days communications were issued instructing all British and American citizens to register. The deadline was noon, December 13.

I was issued a red arm band B (for British) 14/14. This was to be worn at all times under all circumstances, and my name was entered with thousands of others in the logs of the enemy. The bamboo wireless (grapevine gossip) buzzed with speculation, and the words whispered in every drawing room were "concentration camp."

It would take the Japanese almost a year to organize our civilian internment. The so-called "political" prisoners of war were not as fortunate. Under the command of Major General Koneshita, head of the Kampetai (Japanese Special Police) headquarters were set up in a facility called Bridge House. Suspect men were yanked from their offices or homes, day or night, and hauled before his tribunals for accusation and interrogation.

Pain is the rhetoric of brutality, and when the mind cannot be persuaded, the body is—generally through devious and sadistic methods. Bridge House became the horror chamber of the Japanese occupation of Shanghai.

Some seventeen steel barred and bolted "cages" which were to become resonant with the screams of delirium of persistent torture, in both the main building and annex, were the waiting chambers of those about to be "tried" through Koneshita's persuasion.

As many as thirty-five to forty prisoners were often crammed at once into a twenty by nine-foot cage-like cell, all making use of the single bucket in a corner for excrement and reaching for food through a small wicket at the base of the barred door. They slept on the bare boards and helped pick the lice off each other (a record of 500 off a single man in one instance!).

Heroics gave way to insanity and noble men died grotesque deaths. Excerpts from a series of articles written by one of the British survivors of Bridge House, which appeared in the *North China Daily News* after the war, are the most eloquent tribute to those who endured.

For twenty minutes he tried to persuade me to confess, but I continued to deny everything. He then shrugged his shoulders and said that I would have to take the consequences.

One guard was testing an electrical shocking device. I was ordered to sit down at a desk, which I did, when they placed in front of me a piece of paper and pencil and told me that I had ten minutes to write a farewell letter to my wife, as I was going to die. My reply was "If you murder me tonight it is your responsibility and not mine to notify my wife."

One of them savagely struck me across the face for this, but they left the paper and pencil in front of me and started to count off the minutes: nine-eight-seven-six-

five-four-three-two-one.

"Now," they said, "get ready to die."

I knelt for a moment and commended my spirit and prayed for strength. The guards stood by in utter silence while I was doing this. I then lay down on the bench and they proceeded to strap me down. They pulled down my trousers and bared my whole body...

After his body was sprayed with water the electric shock treatment began, with electrodes being applied to all sensitive body parts. As shock after shock convulsed him, he would mercifully pass out, mad with pain, only to be revived with hot coffee for more of the treatment. This was followed by the famous Oriental water treatment. A wet towel was placed across his mouth and nose, and then streams of water were poured on until he had to gulp more and more water to avoid suffocation...

Every now and then the guard who was sitting on my stomach jumped up and down. This forced all the water up into my mouth, but being unable to expel it I had to swallow my own vomit. Again I passed out. When I came to the interpreter began to shriek, "Speak, you bastard, speak!"

He was tortured for six hours; his screams piercing the darkness to penetrate the psyche of the others in the cages, each waiting the call to their own personal Armageddon.

At eight in the morning he was returned to his cell, on the fringe of insanity, where his fellow prisoners wrapped him in a blanket and watched carefully for any signs of his mind breaking. As he would hallucinate and call to imaginary visions of his wife, brother, and mother, they pulled him to his feet, slapped him hard across his face and said, "Don't give up, don't give in. Pull yourself together!"

He made it and survived. Others didn't.

Men were beaten beyond recognition, strung up by their thumbs, shackled and tortured to the brink of death. Occasionally the guards would amuse themselves by shaving off the eyebrows and clipping the eyelashes of a prisoner. One sixty-two-year-old prisoner named Old Pops died shouting "black, white, black, white, up, down, up, down..." and screaming endlessly. Words had been carved into his legs, his wrists were festering where they had been cut by the restraining ropes, and he had been returned to his cell babbling incoherently.

These were the political prisoners of Shanghai.

My father, Lieutenant Ernest William Westwood.

Internment

IN HONG KONG my father was fighting his own bloody battle. A lieutenant with the Royal Navy Volunteer Reserves, he watched the approach of the enemy across the mainland. Barrage and counterbarrage smoked across the hills until they hit the city suburbs of Kowloon and long feathery lanes leaped out of the sea a hundred feet tall.

After ten days of battle action, incisive and clear orders were given: "Blow and destroy all equipment.

Burn and run!" Jolting explosions shook the naval station as rifle butts smashed equipment and high octane gasoline fired the officers' huts and burned confidential records. One man drew his revolver and, waiting for a moment when his dog's attention was diverted, shot him neatly.

Hong Kong fell. After days of gut-level action in the battle of Repulse Bay Hotel, my father was captured and imprisoned. A well-set man, weighing in at about 180 pounds, he weighed ninety pounds after his release.

In Shanghai we stood by for our own imprisonment. The Japanese took months to commandeer the necessary concentration camp compounds. After sorting through their registered, arm-banded lists, they formulated a general plan for segregation and designation. Single men, or those separated from their families, were sent to a prison hellhole across the Whangpoo called Pootung. Here, in unbelievably bad conditions, lacking food, sanitation, and adequate shelter, they scrambled about for themselves and their own mutual survival and managed to clean up, sustain, and survive. Some escaped with dire consequences for those remaining in the camp, and others (Americans who were repatriated under the prisoner exchange) scalded the Japanese through reports to the International Red Cross of the stinking conditions. Most of us were designated "civilian POW."

It was a lousy time for an appendectomy. Our notification had just come from the authorities that we were to report to the grounds of the Cathedral Church for shipment and internment in "Civil

Assembly Center 'C' Yangchow." However you phrased it, it was concentration camp. The dread of the inevitable that had hovered over the British and American communities in Shanghai for months became reality.

The instructions stated that we would each need a camp cot, that we could take in a mosquito net, folding chair, and small trunk which would be transported for us with the cot ahead of time. And then on the day of our assembly at the Cathedral we were allowed to bring only that which we could personally carry. That didn't amount to much for one small woman and a twelve-year-old girl. During the traumas of the notification I suffered an attack of appendicitis and required immediate surgery.

I awakened from the anesthetic with my eyes focused on a little tin can on the nightstand by my hospital bed. It held the offending organ— reminding me that the same malady had caused my brother's death.

The doctor's strong hands patted mine and his authoritative tones assured my mother that all was well and I would be strong and hearty again in a matter of weeks. The imminent question was, however, "How much will she be able to carry into camp?" His unfortunate answer was, "Practically nothing."

My mother had to rely only on her own frail arms to carry for us those life-sustaining items that would tip the weight of balance of our survival in the camp. Of course no one expected our imprisonment to last more than six months—surely by then the Japs would be whipped!

There was an almost festive air around the community in the confidence and assurance that our confinement would be minimal and the Allied war machine would soon vanquish the enemy. Little did we know that our confinement was to last two and a half long and grueling years.

The black market was thriving. Canned goods were at a premium and my mother sold one of her beautiful, large cut-crystal vases in order to purchase two cans of butter. We lined our two small trunks with canned meat, fish, milk, vitamins, and whatever we could purchase that might stretch our health or perhaps our very life a day, a week, or even a month or two longer. Blankets and warm clothing came next. We were instructed to take in tin or enamel plates, cups, knives, forks, spoons, and thermos flasks. We chose two suitcases for my mother to carry. I would manage the thermos flasks and Dog Toby.

Dog Toby was chosen because, of all my toys, he was the one I loved the most. Originally knitted to be a "lamb," somewhere along the line the instructions had gone askew and he had emerged from my mother's flying needles a brown and maroon dog with mutton-chop legs! His wobbly shoe-button eyes and puckered, stitched mouth gave him a doleful expression that said, "Love me, I'm ugly!"

Toby was always lonely, even when surrounded by the other dolls and stuffed animals on my bed. He stood aloof, and perhaps it was my own identity with his loneliness that made him fit so snugly into the contours of my sympathy and love. This was to be his moment of honor and glory.

102

We carefully ripped open the seam down his back and removed all the cotton wool stuffing from his head, legs, and main body. Rolling our paper money into tight wads (it included a wide range of Chinese denominations, for who would know whether or when we would need two dollars or two hundred dollars?) we wrapped the cotton wool around the money and restuffed Toby. As an afterthought, we even managed to squeak another four hundred dollars up his skinny tail!

In a mere half hour, Toby had become a multi-thousand-dollar dog. I was to carry him and he was to be solely my responsibility for the duration of our imprisonment. I could only respond to the gravity of this trust by clutching him to me, kissing him soundly on his tightly stitched mouth, and saying, "We'll be all right, Toby."

Shanghai was a flurry of activity and intrigue as families destined for concentration camps arranged to have Chinese or neutral Swiss friends store their treasures and send them food parcels whenever possible. My mother, through her contacts with B. & S., managed to have a steamer trunk of our valuables stored in one of their go-downs (warehouses), and other friends kept a few of our intimate treasures, among them my Shirley Temple doll and precious baby doll Gloria.

Rickshaws, private cars, some chauffeur driven, and transportation provided by friends all converged at the Cathedral grounds, unloading their cheerful though apprehensive cargoes of heavily laden prisoners. Six hundred of us were destined for

Yangchow Camp "C," and we clustered in small groups, sitting on our suitcases, watching the new arrivals.

The arrival of the Bradley family was the most notable. Mother and Aunt Bradley carried nothing while Father and Uncle Bradley, together with their two strapping teen-age sons, carried between them two long bamboo poles laden with suitcase after suitcase and hamper after hamper, all swinging loosely by their handles. They even carried a gramophone, which was to be the cheer of the camp and uplift of the internees for the duration of the war.

Bamboo is the staple of the Orient. The strong, hollow, and flexible wood has been revered in the Chinese culture for centuries, its beauty an inspiration to Chinese art. Its practical values range from use of the roots as a savory vegetable, to use in conduit irrigation pipe lines, in the manufacture of sturdy furniture and in the crafting of delicate flutes. The ingenuity of the Bradley family led them to harness its potential as a means of transport, and it carried for them all that they would never have been able to carry alone. Why had we not thought of a bamboo pole? The same thought must have reverberated throughout the waiting crowd. But with the help and generosity of this family who generated kindness to all around them, no one was very resentful.

We all smiled somewhat nervously at each other with the realization that we were to be strange bedfellows under stress circumstances for who knew how long: Taipans, accustomed to a retinue

104

of servants, fur-draped socialite women whose hands had never touched a soiled plate, and everyone from the middle-class colonial down to those of questionable repute. There were Russian women who spoke little English but had married Englishmen; Eurasian girls of exceptional beauty, with jet-black Chinese hair, slender oriental bodies, and the fair-skinned, blue-eyed English characteristics; missionaries with black Bibles tucked under their arms, their women in telltale practical shoes with rolled down white socks.

My eyes lit up as we recognized friends, and as I curiously surveyed the gathering crowd I felt that in a sense I was just being born. I was shedding my old life moment by moment, and the excitement and strangeness of a totally new society and environment were spinning a web around me. I found it quite fascinating, and in spite of the many small, strutting Japanese guards hovering about us, I felt absolutely no fear, just a growing curiosity.

It was fitting that we were gathered on consecrated ground. The Cathedral Church had for generations served as the High Church of Shanghai, with all the ritual, pomp, and circumstance of the Episcopalian order. Nobility had bowed their heads and bent their knees to worship there, marriages had been performed, new life had been consecrated, and burials dispatched. Its bell, which normally tolled the call to Sunday services, now tolled for us, and as I saw the black Bibles tucked under several arms, and the swirling skirts of a Jesuit priest, I knew that God was with us.

The roots of faith the nuns had so carefully tended

105

in my young life were wrapped around my entire being, and if there was a fault in the simplicity of my trust it was in that I took God for granted. He was in charge of my soul, my guardian angel hovered over me, Madeleine Sophie and the saints and hosts of heaven were praying for me, and that was that; after all, was I not a child of the Sacred Heart?

Entering into the most impressionable years of my life, I would find the experiences and circumstances of our imprisonment yanking hard on the simplicity of that faith. My growing, questioning mind was to dig deep and stir the soil of my inbred Roman Catholicism.

Unlike most of the internees in Shanghai proper who reported directly to their local camps, we were transported a day and a night's journey up the coast to Chingkiang, to then be transferred from the Japanese steamer to barges. These would take us up a five-hour journey through the famous Grand Canal of the Emperor Shih Huang Ti to Yangchow.

Six hundred of us swarmed onto the ship, and though conditions were crowded, they were not impossible. Indeed the novelty of sleeping with six other women in a small cabin on a Japanese *tatami* mat was a stimulating experience, and by nightfall tempers had settled. The Bradley boys set up their gramophone on the upper deck and the familiar strains of "Stardust" and "Begin the Beguine" dissolved tensions. The Bradleys had brought along about six records, some twelve sides, and they served as our total supply of music, growing fainter and fainter as needles and grooves wore down over the years.

106

That night as our ship churned the muddy waters of the Whangpoo out into the Yellow Sea, I sat clutching Dog Toby, reassured by the hard crinkle of his monetary skeleton, listening to Glenn Miller, Artie Shaw, and Benny Goodman. It was strangely amusing that the roll of drums that sent us to our prison years was beat to "String of Pearls," "I Want to Be Happy," "In the Mood," and "Elmer's Tune."

Observing the adults who paced the deck, talking in monotones punctuated with occasional nervous laughter, it seemed to me that the only constants were the immovable stars of heaven: Orion's Belt, the two dippers, and other patterns of the twinkling night sky. As I gazed into the galaxies that night there was born in me an awe of the greatness of God the Creator. The maneuvers of men seemed insignificant against the vastness of the moon, stars, and Milky Way.

Barges awaited us on the canal, and we began the chaotic transfer, person by person, each loaded with all he could carry. We were packed tighter and tighter into the boats, standing side by side, row by row, spaced only by the suitcases or parcels at our feet. My mother, aunt, and I were fortunate in being situated toward the end of one of the barges. This gave us a little more breathing space and gave me a clear vision of the journey north.

For five hours we stood, occasionally taking turns to rest on the suitcases while others stood, and for the first time I cursed the Japanese. There were no sanitary facilities. Men had the advantage of being able to relieve themselves easily over the rail of the barge while those around discreetly averted their eyes. But sanitation for the women and children soon developed into a major problem, until someone emptied a small tin can of its precious contents. A circle formed facing out—that is, with backs to the can and its occupant. Each time the can was used, the waste was emptied into the canal. It was the beginning of indignity, and my face flushed every time I heard the tinkling use of our self-styled rest room. I constricted my muscles as long as possible, resolved not to submit to this embarrassment, and was mortified when my mother took her turn.

There was a strange silence on the barge, broken only by the lap of the water mile after mile. Mesmerized by the muddy, swirling ebbs I stared into them for endless periods until my mother would nudge me to look at a pagoda or at the peasants standing on the banks of the canal watching our progress.

Overnight, class distinction paled and we had merged into a tired, apprehensive conglomerate of people, leveled by the demands of the basic functions of the human body.

Yangchow

THE CHRISTIAN MISSIONARY compounds
throughout China, with their protective walls,
dormitory facilities, large chapel buildings, dining
halls, and kitchens were ideally suited for
internment camps, and the Japanese
commandeered many of them for this use.

The mission at Yangchow where we were assigned
had been one of the first established in China by
Hudson Taylor in 1868. In Marshall Broomhall's

Jubilee Story of the China Inland Missionary Society he tells of the famous riot of Yangchow which nearly cost Dr. Taylor and his wife their lives. The following excerpt illustrates the difficulties they had in establishing the gospel of Jesus Christ in China.

In regard to riots in China, the long-standing enmity of the literati of China to all things foreign must be remembered as well as the fact that the Chinese people were at that period in the point of superstition very much where we were in the sixteenth century. Should the literati stir up the passions of the people by playing upon their superstitious fears, few officials had the moral courage as well as the ability to keep the peace for long, for their tenure of office was largely dependent upon the goodwill of the scholarly class.

About a fortnight before the storm burst, a meeting of the literati was held in the city, and ere long, anonymous handbills were posted up throughout the city containing many absurd and foul charges. These handbills were followed by large posters calling the foreigners "brigands of the religion of Jesus," and stating that they scooped out the eyes of the dying and opened foundling hospitals in order that they might eat the children.

It was little wonder, after such propaganda, that masses of Chinese stormed the residences of the Taylors, causing them to flee for their lives. Dr. Taylor was badly stoned, and his house was set on fire. His wife and the other missionaries with them had to be lowered from the upper story to escape.

110

(Above) The Christian missionary compounds throughout China were ideally suited for internment camps. We were interned in the Girls' Language School of the mission at Yangchow, first established by Hudson Taylor in 1868.

(Below) The chapel of the Language School served as dorm for many families. D. J. Watson can be seen by the clump of bushes (right) which served as his study.

The mission at Yangchow was established on courageous prayer and soon grew to be the center for Women's Language Study of the C.I.M. It was a beautiful compound with pockets of trees which were to solace our spirits and shade our parched hearts for the duration of our internment. A row of tall, straight poplars divided the upper compound from the lower compound and served as a backdrop for many of our gatherings. I was to spend endless hours weaving in and out through their strong trunks and running my fingers over the design of their beautiful bark. They were living long before I was born and they would possibly still be living long after I was dead. They reached to the heavens, towering over the walls of our confinement, and their greenery held my heart in sanctuary. They were my privacy in a world of voices, close bodies, and hunger.

As we straggled in through the eastern moon gate, an exhausted and defeated entourage toting our suitcases, we assembled to be addressed by the Camp Commandant Hashimoto and our representative Mr. G. (who had been carefully selected by the British Consulate). Even the Bradley boys sagged as they stumbled in with their long pole of suitcases.

"You will not try to escape or your fellow inmates will suffer the consequences of your folly."

"You will be assigned to your dormitories and will elect your own representative to report all grievances to the Central Camp Committee."

"You will be given duties which you will perform."

"You will report for roll call daily."

112

"You will cooperate with all instructions of the Commandant."

"You will ... you will ... you will..." The monotone dragged on and on.

My mother, aunt, and I were assigned to a women's dormitory on the second (top) story of one of the sturdy brick buildings. There were sixty of us in the dorm, and we were each allocated a 6' × 5' space in which to erect our camp bed and place our small trunk. My mother and I placed our beds at the outside edges of our space and set our trunks end on end to form a table, boxing in three sides of our square. Unfortunately we were not quick enough to grab a window or wall space, but were situated in the central area of the room with beds and women all around us. My mother was elected dorm representative to report to the Central Camp Committee.

I sat cross-legged on my camp cot and observed the ménage of women around me. They came from all walks of life and national origins. I was completely fascinated. At a most impressionable period of my young life, I was to be exposed to the emotional tensions of communal living, under stress circumstances that taught me the ascending and descending qualities of the human temperament and spirit.

The men's dorm was down a passageway, and several families shared the few smaller rooms on the lower floor. Sheets of whatever makeshift drapery was available was hurriedly erected to separate families in the smaller rooms and give them a feeble bid at privacy.

113

The dorms had no dividers—the room was a stage open to every tear, giggle, or confrontation. We laughed together, wept together, took sides in quarrels together, and grew to love or hate each other. In my own childish heart I neither loved nor hated but was merely an observer fascinated with the kaleidoscope of human frailty.

My convent modesty demanded that I wiggle in and out of my clothes under the covers, and this became such a trial that within a few weeks I broke down and, following the example of most of the inmates of the dorm, brazenly dressed and undressed in full public view.

Sanitation was a major problem. Each brick building had its own latrine—in our case it consisted of four small cubicles with wooden pail "thunder boxes" to service some one-hundred-thirty or more people. Once a day "moodung" amahs came into the camp swinging huge wooden tubs on either side of a bamboo pole slung across their shoulders. They would then empty our small "moodung" pails into their large tubs and stagger out of the camp with their unsavory loads. I pondered at great length the lot of a "moodung" amah whose life was spent loading and unloading human excrement!

Through the months the "moodung" amahs learned to smile at us, but attempted conversations were soon cut short when we discovered one amah was caught chatting with an inmate, then accused of bringing in news of the outside war. She was severely beaten and forced to kneel in the snow for some hours by the Japanese gatehouse, within the vision of those occupying the chapel dormitories.

Our water supply was dependent upon two pumps in the compound and a covered reservoir into which we placed stored water. Water seemed always in limited supply, and during the summer when the earth could not be coaxed to yield up its life-giving quench, we were rationed to three cups per day for everything. Needless to say we drank, and forewent the rest.

We would line up with our pails, fifty, sixty, two hundred, three hundred of us waiting, and a full pail when one's turn came meant washing. To be able to wash face, body, hair, and clothing—the miracle of a pail of water! The supply was fairly adequate most of the year, but those long, dry summer months meant thirst and dirt.

I cursed my emerging womanhood. We had no sanitary pads and I used a ripped-up towel to catch my monthly flow. As only one towel could be spared to rip up, this meant washing out each sodden rag in limited water with no soap. I vomited through the first few experiences of dealing with my own feminine wastes and found the natural processes of my own body a hateful, shameful experience. Once a month for two and a half years I dealt with my own personal purgatory.

Fortunately Yangchow had a delightful rainy season, and we experienced the joy of a full reservoir, high-yield pumps, and, best of all, rain water running off the gutters into the large Chinese ceramic *kongs* placed at strategic drains. This meant clean hair, clean clothes, clean bodies, and an opportunity to get rid of the bedbugs that spawned in the canvas crevices of our camp cots. A pail of water could be placed for a few minutes under the steam exhaust of one of the kitchen boilers to bring it to the luxury of warm or hot. Scalding water was our defense against the bedbugs.

My mosquito net was the joy of my internment. It was a cloister in a public world. In the daytime it would swing in a huge rolled knot above my bed, and I would kick it with a toe and imagine melodies to its spinning rhythm. At night when it tucked me into solitude, it was my cave, my castle, my secret garden. I fantasized that its mesh was really golden walls or floral arbors, and even in the winter months when nets were discarded for the season, I would insist on retaining mine (much to the derision of the others in the dorm).

On one occasion three other girls and I were asked to dance for the camp's entertainment. Two men donated their mosquito nets for our costumes, and we had flowing gossamer skirts in which to twirl to the melody of "Tales from the Vienna Woods," played on the shaky piano the missionaries had left in the dining hall.

In Yangchow we had seasons—spring, summer, autumn—and winter. During the winter a light snow often covered the frost-bitten ground. We had no heat. This meant sweaters, overcoats, several pairs of socks, gloves, and mittens day and night.

Almost everyone in the camp had chilblains during the winter months. Finger and toe joints would swell, become crimson red, and crack and bleed. In bed at night, snuggled under a covering of practically all my clothing, piled up for warmth, I would feel the chilblains heat up and start itching

116

madly. I would thrust my hands and feet out from under the covers to cool them down, and then as they lost the itch they would ache with the cold. In and out my hands and feet would go all night, and the trick was to try and get to sleep in between the itching and the aching.

In winter we would sit huddled around a hot cup of wishy-washy tea, or water if there was no tea. We sipped it as slowly as possible to warm up our cold interiors and to snatch from the cup a comfort for our cold hands and feet.

The thermos flask was the indispensable utensil of concentration camp life. Hot water was dispensed twice a day, and we each stood in line to have our thermos filled. Mother and I had four thermoses until the horrible day when I broke one. Fortunately, my aunt was in charge of the hot water lines, and if we hurried back to our dorm and quickly used the water in one of our thermoses, we could then run back to the line and she would see to it that it was filled again. This was, of course, when water was not in short supply. When water was rationed the quota was three cups per person per day—no exceptions.

Our food was basic and standard for two and a half years. The morning meal consisted of cracked wheat or *congee* (rice gruel), complete with weevils or maggot-like worms, and the evening meal brought us SOS (Same Old Slop). SOS was an apology of a stew. We were lucky to find two small pieces of pork floating in our bowl of watery soup, and maybe a piece or two of turnip or carrot.

The Yangchow compound had a bakery building,

117

and our men soon became expert at stretching the limited rations the Japanese would send in. They learned to bake excellent bread. True, we only obtained two (or sometimes one) slice per day, but it was good and it was a treat. Occasionally we had larger bread rations and my mother and I would share ours with some of the men in the camp who were obviously suffering from the extremely limited rations. We were small women and did not need as much.

The cans of meat and other foods we had so carefully stashed away at the bottom of our trunks or suitcases were expended within the first few months of our confinement. After all, we thought, "a few short months and the Japs will be whipped!"

The most coveted duty was to be temporarily assigned to the kitchen. This meant women and some children preparing carrots, turnips, or potatoes and men cubing pork from the two sides of a pig sent in daily. The guardhouse would lop off choice cuts of the meat and the problem was stretching the remainder to feed 600! Kitchen duty meant nibbling an extra carrot or slipping one into a pocket for later. In some cases the kitchen helpers even prepared a choice caldron of stew for themselves!

All cooking was done on large Chinese caldrons set in adobe or cement bases. The small opening at the base of the primitive stove was fed dry reeds which had been gathered from the banks of the canal. These were highly inflammable, and great care had to be taken in stoking the fires to avoid a backlash of flames and severe burns.

A squad of teen-age boys organized themselves into a "Stokers" club called the "Night Hawks." They

118   *SOS chow lines—a lesson in fair play as to how many pieces of carrot, or bits of meat, allowed per person.*

ranged in age from fourteen to seventeen and were led by a lithe, personable youth who was given the nickname of Pee-Wee. Not only did they stoke our fires, but most of them at one time or another suffered burns, some quite severely. It was terribly important to make friends with the stokers, as that meant extra hot water or the extra odd munch on a carrot. It became customary for the stokers to whittle delicate initial brooches out of privet wood or any other decent-sized branch they could take from one of the compound trees. It was a great thrill for me to be one of the few girls selected to receive one of these brooches.

Three times during the two-and-a-half years of our confinement we received Red Cross parcels—twice from the American Red Cross and once from the Canadian Red Cross. These were golden days, filled with shouts of glee, especially from the children. The internees were delighted to discover slabs of vitamin-enriched chocolate, cans of "Klim" (powdered milk), Spam, and cigarettes.

Cigarettes became the great monetary exchange. Smokers in the camp were eager to trade their chocolate or Klim for a few packs, and it became quite a moral choice for the missionaries to decide whether it was spiritually kosher to feed a man's vice in order to nourish a child's body. Just what the missionaries did with their cigarettes, I never did find out. My mother and I were quick to exchange ours—hers for Klim and mine for chocolate, which we rationed out to ourselves and held in our mouths for as long as possible!

The Qualities of Privation

INNOVATION became our lifeline, and the ingenuity that was harnessed during our internment affirmed the old adage, "Necessity is the father of invention." A search for talent, skill, and adaptability was continually being conducted over the camp, and all available know-how was directed toward the common good. The indomitable British spirit set its jaw and said, "We'll manage—somehow." And we did!

A man who had mended boots during the First
World War became the camp cobbler—he
stretched, stitched, swapped, and patched our
shoes, and, to accommodate the feet of growing
children, he simply cut out the tips of our shoes and
let our toes dangle. One of the women got the clever
idea of braiding strips of cloth (torn from the hems of
clothing, or in some instances, from ripping up an
entire garment) into firm soles, and then stitching
fabric thongs across the tops. These made rather
pretty sandals for both boys and girls. Winter, of
course, was a problem, and then leather shoes simply
had to be patched, extended through toe or heel, and
repatched.

As my curves developed, my mother let out all
the seams that she could. The Peter Pan-collared
and smocked dresses that Sung the tailor had
made for me at twelve or thirteen looked pretty
ridiculous on me at fifteen and a half! Skirts and
blouses were a godsend, as skirts could be worn slung
low to make them longer and blouses worn outside
for more growth room. Being a "little" girl, I did
not fare as badly as some of the taller girls who
seemed to shoot up overnight and suddenly need
to share their mothers' limited clothing. Teen-age
boys had an even worse problem. Their short pants
got shorter and their long pants suddenly became
short pants. None of us got fatter—all of us got
thinner—which had its compensations in
providing the necessary growing room.

Sweaters were unraveled to make several pairs
of mittens for our swollen chilblained hands, and a
round robin of shared services circled and touched

each of our lives. Just as there were workers and shirkers, there were givers and takers. Adversity was either the cancer that crippled the human spirit, or the challenge that lifted its character to new heights of nobility.

The password to most solutions was "make-do," generally preceded by a great big sigh. "That was the last of the tooth powder? Well (sigh), we'll just have to *make-do* without it!"

Occasionally the SOS (Same Old Stew) ran out before those at the end of the food queue had been served, in which case those left hungry just had to "make-do" (sigh) and be the first ones served, with an extra portion to boot, at the next meal!

There were three chow calls, one for each of the three sections of the alphabet. As Westwoods we had to wait for the third call, which put us in a disadvantaged position until the camp committee decided to reverse the order of calls in the interest of fair play. After running out of food a few times, the servers became more cautious in serving the first-comers, which often meant that the final section got a more generous ladle! Apportioning the caldrons of stew (served in wooden buckets) to a community of 600 was no slight task, and it seemed that the servers were criticized however they handled it.

Morale was high, and with the exception of a few ebb tides, remained high for the duration of the confinement. Probably 80 percent of the internees pitched in to do their bit cheerfully.

Humor was the neutralizer of tension. There were a couple of excellent cartoonists in the camp, and periodically a well-timed quip, duly illustrated, would appear on the makeshift bulletin board outside the dining room. We shared their jokes about overflowing latrines, the "natural blond" who now had jet black hair, how to take a complete bath in one mug of water, the nutritive value of the strange objects occasionally found in the stew ... on and on. Our spirits were cheered and it seemed that when things were the toughest, humor was the highest. It was either laugh, or shrivel up in self-pity.

A typical birthday present was perhaps half a bar of soap given by a friend—soap became one of the most valuable items in the camp as the months wore on. I recall the second birthday I celebrated in camp. One of the Night Hawks gave me a full bar of soap and a whittled brooch bearing my initials. He was terribly disappointed as at the last moments of the carving one of the bars of the letter "F" had broken off.

I lay on my bed, fingering the brooch, and kicked my knotted-up mosquito net. I remembered past birthdays. Gala fancy dress parties, attended by a full retinue of servants. Bowls and bowls of strawberries with fresh whipped cream, finger sandwiches, and a huge cake ordered especially for the occasion from Bianca's, the famous bakery on Bubbling Well Road!

I kissed the simple birthday card my mother had traced for me and caught the salty tears with the tip of my tongue as they rolled down my cheeks to the corners of my mouth.

I thought a lot about food. On the days when the supplies did not come in and we were rationed to one turnip, I'd imagine myself at one of our family banquets at Sun Ya's, my teeth crunching into bamboo shoots and Peking duck. At times like that, pacing around the perimeter of the camp wall to walk off frustrations seemed the only answer.

From the first weeks of settling into camp routine, children were included in the assignment of duties. For the most part the boys hauled buckets of water and stoked the fires (like the Night Hawks). The girls swept floors, peeled potatoes and carrots, or served on hospital duty. It was essential that our time be ordered and disciplined to fend off the depressing circumstances of our confinement.

Within a month an exceptionally staffed and equipped school was set up by a remarkable teacher, the sister of the headmistress of one of Shanghai's leading girls' schools. Whether she had the foresight and commitment to use her limited trunk space to include a few choice textbooks, copybooks, pens, and pencils, or whether the Red Cross had furnished her with basic equipment, I don't know. But within a few short weeks she had registered all missionary teachers in the camp as well as volunteers whose backgrounds or professions qualified them to serve. Indeed, we were most fortunate in having interned with us many of the excellent teachers from China's missionary schools.

In strict British tradition, the girls were separated from the boys (with one exception—the sixth grade had only one girl, who joined the boys) and children were graded according to age. We made use of the long tables in the dining hall for our makeshift classroom. It demanded super concentration as teachers tried to keep their voices quiet so as not to interfere with each other, and students strained to catch information without being diverted by what was going on at the next table. The fifth and sixth grades were assigned to a small guardhouse, normally out of bounds to internees, through special permission of the Commandant.

A full and rich curriculum was offered: French, Latin, arithmetic, algebra, geometry, history, geography, science (with an emphasis on botany due to lack of equipment), English composition, dictation, and literature.

A prominent businessman and accountant taught higher mathematics to the upper grades and fired and dazzled his students by teaching them shortcuts, such as multiplying five or more digits by five or more digits on a single line. We went through British history from the Elizabethan era to the Norman Conquest and the Doomsday Book. We explored the formative period of English Literature (1066-1400) and on to Bacon, Milton, Keats, along with paraphrases of Shakespeare. Our geography lessons, taught by a Canadian, took us twice around Canada.

With no student textbooks, we had to write everything down in our limited supply of copybooks. We were cautioned from the very beginning to save space wherever possible, and that we did. But as our supply of copybooks ran out after the first year, we wrote smaller and smaller and eventually drew lines in between the lines until each page became tightly packed with script. The backs of tin can labels or any scraps of paper were saved and used—even the coarse brown toilet paper the Japanese sent in was used for schoolwork toward the end of our internment.

Our pencils, pens, and ink were rationed. Eventually our pencils became stubs, and a lost pencil became a disaster. Stealing a pencil stub was cause to be hauled up before the School Committee.

Examinations were held and graded, and reports furnished to parents. Every subject was enriched by the fact that teachers could give extra time to us. We were also blessed by the company of some great intellects interned with us. Travelers gave reports on countries they had visited, and these firsthand experiences overshadowed textbook details, enlarging our student world to fascinating proportions. It was an education *summa cum laude!*

Without the stimuli of radio, movies, or other outside entertainment media, I thought a great deal and read a great deal. We obtained books from the little library organized from Red Cross supplies and campers' book contributions. Cut off from the world for two and a half formative years, I was left to get to know my own thoughts and to think thoughts worth knowing. I analyzed the abnormalities of the strange society confined within our walls: I became a people watcher.

Physical recreation was a necessity. Out of the blue a softball bat, a couple of gloves, and balls showed up, and in the nice weather softball became the favorite sport of all age levels. We were fortunate in having a good-sized field by the back wall as well as a smaller quadrangle in the front on

127

which to play and take our exercise. I pitched for the "Cucumbers" and struck out a lot at bat until I learned how to bunt!

The men had competitive teams, augmented by one girl who was a whiz at sports. For diversion, it was decided that the team which lost the series would be required to shave their heads—which gave added impetus to the game and spirit to the cheering squads. Katie's team lost and she went through a period of horrible teasing as her hair was threatened. Mercifully, she was spared the razor, but hoots of laughter accompanied each of her team members as they took their turn in full public view to be completely shorn! They did look funny and they provided us with much-needed hilarity through several months as we watched their hair slowly grow in, inch by stubbly inch.

The Japanese guards observed all of this, occasionally leaning on their rifles and smiling. On the whole they did not bother us, provided we obeyed all the regulations and were subdued. Once they did interfere when one of the men was giving a lecture. He drew a map on the dining room blackboard showing several islands in the Pacific. It was an innocent act—he was merely lecturing about his travels. But the Japanese guard on duty feared the man was involved in war maneuvers; he had him hauled into the guardhouse and put him through the third degree! We were very careful after that.

Katie and her fiancé Monty, a handsome, swashbuckling man, decided that the war was dragging on, and on, and on, with no end in sight.

They wanted to get married. Katie was coach of the girls' softball team and was a great favorite among all the kids. Monty led the men's dorm in roll call each morning, the thirty or so men snapping to attention as they boomed out their count in Japanese "*ichie, nee, san, chi....*"

Everyone was jubilant when Katie and Monty received permission from the Camp Committee and the Commandant. Theirs was a popular match, and their wedding plans sent a ripple of excitement through an emotionally and physically tired people.

Bits of veil, scraps of choice fabric, and greens from the camp trees were gathered. A small storage room, about 10' × 10', was emptied and given to the couple for their honeymoon. It would hold at least their beds, trunks, and camp chairs, and provide the necessary privacy. The Night Hawks and adoring children of the camp took turns at standing in the food queues to get their meals. The marriage took place in a simple service conducted by the Roman Catholic priest.

We had one marriage, one birth, and two deaths during our internment. All four events took place in the last year. Tragically, one of the young Night Hawks was stricken and died. The horrible rumor of "cholera" was whispered about and then quickly stifled. Fortunately the camp did not suffer devastating epidemics. Dysentery was the main scourge, and few escaped it entirely. There was one case of typhus, quickly isolated in the hospital. Had it spread it would have spelled disaster.

We never knew for sure what took the young Night Hawk. He was buried simply by his mother

129

and father in the small graveyard outside the chapel wall which held the graves of missionaries of C.I.M. and perhaps a few Chinese Christians. It was sanctified ground, for his body lay in the company of saints.

The mighty Emperor of the Island of the Sun could not erase the calendar, and we celebrated our festivals on schedule. Christmas and Easter brought renewed hope with communal services held in the dining hall. The familiar strains of "Silent Night" or "Christ the Lord Is Risen Today" wafted through the camp, and women would hug each other tenderly with tear-filled eyes. The men extended a firm handclasp and gave a thump on the back to exchange greetings of "Buck up, the bloody war has to end sometime!"

Families retreated in reflective silence as thoughts spanned miles to loved ones fighting in the Battle of Britain or trapped in the prisons in Hong Kong, mainland China, or Japan.

The second Christmas of our internment the Camp Central Committee asked the Japanese if we could go meatless for two weeks and then be sent in the meat we had saved for a Christmas meal. The Commandant agreed and somehow we struggled through the stew made of just a minimum of carrots, potatoes, and turnips, looking forward to biting into a sizable piece of pork rather than the odd little cube we occasionally found floating around in our portion (if we were lucky).

The great and glorious day of meat finally came, and the camp cooks did us proud! One cup full of savory cubed pork per person—Happy Christmas!

130

We discovered our taste buds, though dormant, were not dead—they were readily activated and satisfied at least for that one meal in our two-and-a-half-year imprisonment.

I had come a long way from the traditions of the Sacred Heart. At the start of the Advent season in the convent each child was assigned a small white celluloid lamb. In a corner of the central foyer, outside the massive chapel doors, a beautiful crèche was erected on a papier-mâché hillside with potted ferns and simulated rocks. The figure of the infant Christ was draped and covered with purple. Our individual little lambs were all lined up at the far edge of a grassy runway to move forward day by day through merit points for academics, politeness, kindness, and other behavioral achievements. Finally, at the eve of our Christmas vacation, the winning little lamb was selected for the honor of uncovering the babe.

A candlelit procession of white veiled, black stockinged little girls, each holding her own luminary, would circle down the main staircase singing "Angels We Have Heard on High," "Gloria in Excelsis Dei..." Then, in a hushed, awesome ceremony, the infant would be uncovered by the honored student, hugs and kisses would be exchanged, and we'd be dismissed with a final benediction.

My little lamb never quite made it all the way up the hill, let alone to the feet of the Savior. I wondered if this little lamb would make it all the way through prison camp.

My heart heavy with memory, I stepped out into

131

the cold and looked up at a dark night sky tinseled with stars. "The Word was made flesh and dwelt among us," I whispered as I wrapped my cracked, chilblained hands tightly around my tin mug of tea, trying to eke out a bit of warmth.

"Gloria in Excelsis Dei ... On earth peace, goodwill toward men!"

"God," I hissed through clenched teeth, "God, where are you?"

Saints & Sinners

THE CAMP was a complex cultural and social diversity. Women of ill repute rubbed shoulders with the aristocracy; taipans, doctors, and other professional men stood in the food queues with gamblers, knaves, clergymen, and children. Missionaries committed to bringing the gospel of Jesus Christ to the heathen Chinese suddenly found themselves in the midst of a hurting, cantankerous, often sullen and selfish people, who presented them

133

with endless challenges and opportunities to exercise the practicalities of their faith.

One missionary doctor was outstanding in his service. A tall handsome man with mild gray eyes, he had a reputation as one of the best surgeons in the Orient. He did not talk much and I never heard him preach, but he was frequently seen cleaning out the latrines—exposing to the body wastes of the camp his hands that had previously wielded the delicate instruments of healing.

A fairly adequate hospital had been set up on the camp grounds, with two missionary doctors and another doctor and several nurses in charge. They had been permitted to bring in a certain amount of medical supplies and ran a fairly efficient open clinic. It was a tribute to their skill that on occasion even our Japanese guards visited them for treatment. In our isolated outpost, the Japanese were as far removed from their facilities as we were.

As a teen-ager I served several rounds of camp duty, scrubbing the hospital floors or carrying around trays of food. My observation of these remarkable doctors and nurses, working under such limited conditions, made me acutely aware of the resourcefulness of human instinct.

Hospital duty was a coveted chore, as it meant an access to the leftovers of the specially prepared food. Here again, the better, leaner parts of the sides of pork were always removed for the sick before the camp cooking was done. The hospital meant cleanliness, and *moodungs* with room to spare! I almost wished I were sick. Indeed, I did develop dysentery and spent a few days in the luxury of the

134

hospital, which was one of the joyful highlights of my internment.

As medical supplies dwindled and our bodies became anemic, infections became more and more frequent. I had a most uncomfortable time with a huge boil on the nape of my neck, as well as a badly infected heel which refused to heal. But fortunately these occurred toward the end of our internment and our release, and my subsequent treatment with shots of penicillin by the U. S. Army Medical Corps soon fixed me up. What we would have given for penicillin or sulfa or other healing supplies during the war.

The saintly ministrations of our missionary camp doctors were a complement to their faith. They ministered not only to us, their fellow inmates, but to the guards of the enemy as well. "Love your enemies," Jesus had said.

The gambling clique set up headquarters in a small room, amusingly tagged "recreation," and spent the duration of their imprisonment huddled over card games and tallying up the I.O.U. payoffs of their daily wagers. I was told never to go into that room. Several times I lingered outside and caught glimpses of the men of sin as the door swung open or shut, and when I saw the same men walking around the camp or standing in the food queues my eyes would grow wide with curiosity.

I remember the day a missionary couple found their small eight-year-old son in the "gamblers' den," and I think the whole camp remembers the howls from the thrashing he got as a result! On the whole, the gamblers were silent, sallow men who never

135

seemed to be without cigarettes.

I carried my own weight of sin. We tried to break the monotony of our ordeal by entertaining ourselves whenever we could. Having been trained in the dance at the Audrey King Ballet Studio, I was frequently called upon to perform. Scarves, ribbons, or a nightgown or two were loaned for the occasion, and we managed some rather pretty costumes from the scant offerings available.

One of the women at the camp taught me the hula and I swung and swerved my hips through many performances. The beautiful interpretative hand movements—rain, mountain, moon, sea, waves, and the rhythmic roll of the feet, knees, and hips made this one of my favorite dances. Minus a grass skirt, I wrapped myself in a makeshift sarong and swung myself into encores and round after round of applause. Apparently I also swung myself into lust in the hearts of the Night Hawks and other young men of the camp, or so I was told, and I was the recipient of worried glances from several of the missionaries on the morning after a performance.

I did a wild interpretation to "In a Persian Market," dressed in cut-down nightie pantaloons and a covered borrowed bra which, although too large for me, was easily padded with several handkerchiefs. My undulations as a harem girl, with snake charmer arms and the whipping foot motions of the street vendors, brought me even more popularity and acclaim, and apparently generated even more lust, because I was met with more worried glances and sour looks from missionaries on the morning after *that* performance. I started to dislike the missionaries!

136

In contrast to their judgments were the encouragements of the more social internees. "You have great talent, Fay," said a man with show business experience. "You should consider dancing professionally."

Fortunately, about that time, God placed a man of giant spiritual stature before me and gave him the discernment and compassion to reach into the confused heart of this disgruntled teen-ager.

Apparently the prayers of the sisters of the Sacred Heart, the intercessions of Saint Madeleine Sophie and the hosts of heaven, followed by the thrust of the prayers of the camp missionaries as they lifted my wayward talents to heaven and prayed for my purity, moved the hand of the Almighty.

The Jews in the camp held their weekly meetings in the dining hall on Saturdays, the Roman Catholic priests served mass on a makeshift altar in the dining hall early on Sunday mornings, and the Protestant chaplains and missionaries combined in a worship service in the dining hall later on Sunday mornings.

I would sit on the concrete ledge atop a side wall of the water reservoir (which was adjacent to the dining hall) and contemplate the parade of faith. "A bunch of ballyhoo," I thought.

Meanwhile, this man of giant spiritual stature was in turn contemplating me! Not only contemplating me in his mind, but also in his heart and in his prayers before God, his Father.

D. J. Watson went out to China in the early 1930s under the auspices of the London Missionary Society. He was assigned to the Central China countryside surrounding Hangkow, 600 miles inland from Shanghai. Battling Chinese brigands and raids (of what was then an embryo Communist army), his faith had withstood oppressions, physical affronts, and dangers, and he had earned the love and respect of the Chinese people. Training and discipling small teams of native evangelists and living alongside them helped him relate the practicality of the gospel of Jesus Christ to their daily lives. It was a gospel that endured and survived adversity, and we believe the seeds of it still endure and survive despite the Communist onslaught in China today.

Watson was witty, with a merry twinkle in his penetrating blue eyes. He taught history in the camp school, and, indeed, history soon became my favorite subject. In reviewing the ancient lore of the Vikings, the invasions of Britain by the Picts and the Scots, and the foundations of the Magna Carta, we became good friends.

As both our surnames started with "W," we shared the same group call to meals. I soon made it a point of trying to jostle myself into a position behind him in the food queues. Here we could further develop a thought begun in the class discussions, and it gratified me that despite what he called my "atrocious spelling," he thought highly enough of my history essays to take a personal interest in me. It did not then occur to me that his personal interest was spiritually motivated.

Better still, he never criticized my dancing! I was eventually to find out—many years and much spiritual growth later—just what he did think, but he chose not to lay a further hurt on my already confused and angry heart.

The beautiful garnishings of my convent-bred faith in God had wilted in the scorching reality of concentration camp life. The possibility of instant death cast its shadow over each daily roll call, and the blinding beam of a guard's nightwatch torch, as it occasionally invaded the sleeping dorm, tensed muscles and froze spirits. I was not afraid of death, the fact; I was only afraid of dying, the act.

On the whole our captors left us pretty much alone, provided we obeyed all the regulations and roll calls. There were a couple of commandants who were more aggressive, and the fright of being hauled out of bed in the middle of the night to be counted, or the interminable standing in the snow with cracked, chilblained feet, and eyes cast down while the guards gave us a closer line-by-line inspection, placed its brand of terror, confusion, and hate upon me. You grow up fast in war.

Ah-Nee's comforting pat, the tender care of Soeur Cecile were in another lifetime. The "dear sweet Jesus" of my communion prayers, the heavenly strains of the chapel choir, the confessions, rosaries, and liturgies merged into a hallucinatory haze with Saint Therese, the statue of the Sacred Heart of Jesus, and the second-story chapel of the Annunciation of the Blessed Virgin Mary dispersing slowly like a ground mist in the brilliance of the rising sun of Japanese imprisonment. I decided not to believe in God.

I felt alone, bereft and bewildered. I involuntarily performed the behaviors expected of me and continued to attend early mass and steel my heart against truly being touched by God's love.

D. J. Watson confronted me one day in the food queue.

"Are you happy in your faith, Fay?"

"Why?"

"Well, I've been noticing you lately and you've seemed a bit edgy."

Silence.

"Have you read the Gospels—Matthew, Mark, Luke, and John?"

"No," I replied, but added defensively, "I've studied my catechism and know my Bible stories." The last thing I wanted was to have more religious bilge thrust down my parched throat!

"Well," he said, "that's not exactly the same. How would you like to join a little Bible study group I'm starting with one or two of the other girls?"

I had never studied the Bible from the Bible. Indeed I could not remember ever seeing an open Bible. I had my missal and catechism book and had read the lives of many of the saints, but all the Bible stories had been interpreted for us in the convent in simple form. Now here was a man offering me direct rather than secondhand access to the Scriptures. It was an intriguing invitation.

Within the week I could be seen, together with three others, sitting in the grass behind a small group of shrubs, studying the Gospel of John with Rev. Watson.

As though to reinforce this spiritual impact upon my life, there arrived in the camp a new family, transferred from another city. Not only a new family, but a brand new boy with flaming red hair,

140

steady blue eyes, bowed legs, freckles, and an Adam's apple that bobbed up and down when he talked. He carried a large black Bible, and I eyed him curiously. His missionary parents were active in the Native Evangelistic Crusades. He had a beautiful older sister who soon won everyone over, including me, with the sweetness of her nature and kind, tender ways. I set my fifteen-year-old cap for Derek, and there began a friendship and romance that bumped its way through the traumas of many years.

Not only was I getting involved with Saint John the apostle every Tuesday afternoon, but I was getting involved with Saint Paul, Saint James, and just about every other New Testament saint on a continuing basis. Not to mention the redheaded *living* saint who had joined our group. The prime irritant for a sinner is an adjacent saint!

Derek was brilliant at math and, being a couple of years older than I, he offered to coach me as I stumbled through algebra and geometry. It soon became a common sight for us to be sitting together at the back compound wall, puzzling over equations. Somehow he always managed to tuck his Bible into these sessions and spring his wretched verses when all the while I was looking at the contours of his mouth and wondering what it would be like to kiss him!

Terry had taught me a few things from the pictures under the tuck shop counter; Keith and I had done a lot of kissing between tangos; I was accustomed to the teasing quips and whistles of the Night Hawks. But here was Derek, who quickly averted his eyes if they by chance wandered over my

141

developing anatomy, and spoke of himself as the "temple of the Holy Ghost"! He was as straight as the gate and as narrow as the path of the gospel he preached.

I tried to think of him as a dullard or a clod, but my attraction to his strong faith tumbled my resentments. He knew what he believed; he knew in whom he believed; and indeed he seemed to know the directives of his life and to be totally relaxed about the traumas of his present confinement! His trust was in a power mightier than the Japanese guards, the American army, or even the Britannia that ruled the waves. He never flinched or wavered in that trust even though his gangly frame got thinner and thinner as the months rolled along and his Adam's apple stuck out more and more, and hollows developed under his prominent cheekbones.

Best of all, he chose me to be a regular companion, and as our friendship grew I playfully tagged him with the nickname of "Dobbs." Increasingly, I found myself lying under my mosquito net thinking about him, and daydreaming about walking hand in hand down wooded lanes with him, his burning passion breaking down his reserves of self-control. We were falling very much in love.

It was the custom of internees to take their exercise by walking around and around the compound wall, skirting the two gate areas which were forbidden territory. Privacy was an impossibility in the close confinements of our quarters, and intimate conversations were generally held "on the walk." Sitting on our folding canvas camp chairs at the back wall, we had a constant parade of walkers

142

crossing in front of us, which was very unsatisfactory when trying to carry on a flirtation. Also, carrying on a flirtation with a willing sinner was one thing; flirting with a reluctant saint was another! One thing I noticed. The missionaries walking across our path no longer looked worriedly at me, but started smiling. They approved of my companion and his large black Bible.

I saw to it that my hair brushed his cheek as he bent over a theorem, and occasionally his pencil would twist up through my curls and his steady gaze would hold me for a lingering moment.

It was during one of these times of study at the back wall that we saw *the guard.* He was walking up and down the wide rim of the city wall which ran parallel to the compound wall. Whether he had seen us with Dobbs' large black Bible, we don't know, but suddenly he quietly started singing in Japanese to the tune of "Onward Christian Soldiers." As his confidence grew, he sang louder and louder until he reached a triumphant crescendo, and then he stopped, just as suddenly as he had begun, and continued his slow monotonous pacing in silence.

"Do you think he's a Christian, Dobbs?"

"I don't know. Maybe he went to a missionary school in Japan. Maybe he just heard the tune from a church and put his own Japanese words to it."

"Maybe he's trying to tell us something! Maybe he's trying to encourage us!"

"I know," said Dobbs. "He's a sign from God that we're going to be all right!"

As usual, Dobbs had the last word, and I was

content in the assurance that he had it on confidential information direct from his God that we were going to be all right!

My Roman Catholic roots had bred in me an overwhelming awe for the omnipotent transcendency of the Kingship of God. Now my exposure to the Scriptures with D. J. Watson, and to the charisma of a living faith in Dobbs, showed me a personalized God—a God I could come to know intimately, a Father God, a friend God, a God who would not only never leave me or forsake me, but would dwell *in* me!

To top it off, news of my open heart and searching mind must have buzzed around the missionary grapevine, for one day a tall, straight up and down pigtailed daughter of missionaries came up to me and gave me her Bible. She had pasted a small square of paper over her name on the title page and had incribed it in careful print:

> To Fay,
> from Carol
>
> Camp "C" Yangchow—31st of May, 1945
> "Thy Word is a lamp unto my feet
> and a light unto my path"
> (*Psalm 119:105*)

To give away what must have been her own most precious personal possession was an act of love I could only grope to understand. Moreover, since it was her own personal Bible, it contained her notations in the margins. On the back page of the Bible, she had noted:

144

"And grieve not the Holy Spirit of God, whereby ye are sealed unto the day of redemption" (Ephesians 4:30). Grieve is a love word. You cannot grieve one who does not love you. You can hurt or anger him but you cannot grieve him. To grieve the Holy Spirit means that we are causing pain to someone who loves us. What then in us causes this divine One grief?

He is the Spirit of truth (John 14:17), so anything false, deceitful, or hypocritical grieves him.

He is the Spirit of faith (2 Corinthians 4:13), so doubt, unbelief, distrust, worry, anxiety grieve him.

He is the Spirit of grace (Hebrews 10:29), so that which is hard, bitter, ungracious, unthankful, malicious, unforgiving, or unloving grieves him.

He is the Spirit of holiness (Romans 1:4), so anything unclean, defiling, or degrading grieves him.

He is the Spirit of wisdom (and revelation, Ephesians 1:17), so ignorance, conceit, arrogance, and folly grieve him.

He is the Spirit of power, love, and discipline (2 Timothy 1:7), so that which is barren, fruitless, disorderly, confused, and uncontrolled grieves him.

He is the Spirit of glory (1 Peter 4:14), so anything worldly, earthly, or fleshly grieves him.

He dwells within us to enable us "to grow up into Christ in all things" (Ephesians 4:15).

I had grieved him on all counts.

I had grieved him in *truth* by turning my back on the teachings of my childhood under the care of the Sisters of the Sacred Heart; I had grieved him in *faith* by deciding not to believe in God anymore at a time when I needed him the most; I had grieved him in *grace* by developing a bitter spirit; I had grieved him in *holiness* by all the defiling thoughts I constantly entertained; I had grieved him in *wisdom* and *revelation* by being arrogant and foolish; I had grieved him in *power, love,* and *discipline* by being totally confused and spiritually barren and fruitless; and I had grieved him in *glory* by my earthly, worldly attitudes and the rejection of the sweet simplicity of the attitudes of my first Holy Communion.

God had sent me the Scriptures—even placed into my hands a copy of them to keep as my own, in a place where they were completely unobtainable. God had put his teacher, D. J. Watson, into my life; God had brought Dobbs with his confident living faith to carry me along; and God had even placed a Japanese guard singing to the tune of "Onward Christian Soldiers" in front of my eyes!

The magnitude of God's mercy, his patience, his compassion, and his love burst my heart, and I ran in a flood of tears to the solace of D. J. and sobbed out my broken heart on his shoulder. We knelt in the grass of that prison camp and the hand of the Almighty reached down and wrapped itself around my life.

As my tears spattered down to spot the dry, parched earth beneath our knees, the walls of that C.I.M. compound must have shouted their hallelujah—they had been built and sanctified for this very purpose. Hudson Taylor would have been very pleased!

Dobbs was jubilant—he beamed from ear to ear, stretching his freckles until they merged into one huge spot on his cheeks!

That Sunday, I sat in the Protestant service in the dining hall, listened to D. J. preach, and joined in Holy Communion with the believers. We had no bread to break, but we did share the cup—weak, super-diluted tea. It was the elixir of immortality to me, and once again the tears rolled down my pale cheeks.

It was a week past my sixteenth birthday. We had been in camp just over two years.

V-J

ONE DAY two Japanese guards carrying pails of white
paint and ladders climbed onto the roofs of our
buildings and painted POW in huge letters. During
morning roll calls we were told to keep our eyes cast
down to the ground, and we sometimes heard the
faint hum of planes passing overhead. The Red
Cross sent in letters from Chinese or neutral friends
outside the camp which carried secret codes such as
"Cousin Ti has graduated" (in reality there was no

149

cousin Ti—it meant that the Allies had won
another victory).

We learned the art of reading between the lines
of the propaganda newspapers posted on the
bulletin board. Sometimes small groups of men
would gather and analyze the possibilities of victory
and release. Our rations were cut, and then cut
again. The guards and Commandant looked
worried, but this did not hinder them from strutting
around and emphasizing their authority over us.
Everyone was restless.

"Yokomoto will probably commit *hara-kiri*," said
Dobbs thoughtfully.

"In front of all of us?" I inquired.

"Hum-m-m," Dobbs brooded, "maybe!"

"Gosh!" Half of me hoped that he would and the
other half hoped that he wouldn't. I was in awe of
the sacred rite of disembowelment: to die with
honor rather than surrender with dishonor. I
shuddered and wondered whether Yokomoto had a
wife and children. Hashimoto, we had deduced,
must have had children. On one occasion, to
celebrate the Japanese Children's Festival, he had
sent the children of the camp boxes of "moochies"
(small Japanese cakes). It was a touching gesture,
and, as we had nothing sweet in our camp diet, it
was an enormous treat. We had thought then that he
probably missed his own children in Japan.

We clung together in desperate apprehension.
What would the Japanese do to us? The charters of
the International Red Cross protected prisoners of
war, and we all felt sure that our Commandant
would respect those charters since he had been in

150

direct contact with the Red Cross through our Central Camp Committee. But war is fickle and vindictive. Would we be the target of vengeance?

D. J. intensified his Bible studies—we covered more and more material. Suddenly it seemed as though he was racing against time and, before our liberation, wanted to instruct us in the way of faith. We whizzed through Mark and over to the first epistle of John, the beloved. We learned assurances of our faith and cautions against false leaders and trends. We had questions, answers; questions, explanations; and always his prayers for our spiritual growth.

After one such study session D. J. pressed into my hand a small book, *A Devotional Diary,* published by the Student Christian Movement Press in London. He had written in the front:

Expect great things from God,
Attempt great things for God.   WILLIAM CAREY

He had written in the back:

Forth in Thy name, O Lord, I go,
My daily labor to pursue,
Thee, only Thee, resolved to know
In all I think, or say, or do.   CHARLES WESLEY

"My address is here, dear lassie, in care of the London Missionary Society, Westminster, London," he wrote. He also gave a temporary Shanghai address on Yuen Ming Yuen Road.

Along with those others whose lives he touched, I had become his daughter in the Lord, Fairy Fay,

151

beloved in the fellowship of believers.

"Use this little book for your daily devotions and remember, Fay, I will be praying for you always."

On a separate piece of paper he had written out a verse by his good friend Jack Hoyland of the Society of Friends in Birmingham:

O live in us this day,
O clothe Thyself, thy purpose yet again
In human clay;
Work through our feebleness Thy strength,
Work through our meanness Thy nobility,
Work through our helpless poverty of soul
Thy grace, Thy glory and Thy love.

And finally, "Be kind to Dobbs, he is so very fond of you."

Yes, I knew how "very fond" of me he was and took advantage of that fondness whenever I could! We walked around the camp wall each evening, talking about where we would go once we got "outside," and pledging our friendship to each other and the fact that we *must* keep in touch. Then one night, just before the curfew, he pulled me into the shadows behind one of the houses and took me in his arms. "I love you, Fay. I can't hold it back any longer. I love you!"

It was as though his very heart had burst and as we kissed I knew the joy of his unleashed passion. After months of restraint, prayerful consideration, and inward battle, he decided he could not let me go from the cloister of our confinement into the swarming world without his pledge of devotion.

152

It was good to know that holy men were *men* and their holiness did not mitigate their desire. He was so thin that the bones of his rib cage bit into me as he pressed me close to him. I felt the burning of his body and I whispered, "Is it sin to want each other, Dobbs?"

"No," he whispered back, "it is not sin to want each other, but to have each other, that would be sin."

"Do you want me, Dobbs?"

"Yes," he strangled out in a twisted voice, "someday if it is God's will."

I glowed in the knowledge that I was desirable, and wrapped my arms around him, burying my head against his flaming hair. The months of brushing my curls against his cheek at the back wall, the months of his carefully averted eyes, the months of teasing and flirting all exploded! I loved the feel of his arms holding me and his fierce possessive kisses on the nape of my neck. We were in love; nothing else mattered.

If Yokomoto committed *hara-kiri* in front of us, so what; if the Japanese machine-gunned us down, so what; if we starved the rest of the war, so what? These moments were ours, to find each other. I knew that I loved and was loved.

The war had ended two weeks before and we did not know it. Somehow we had become a lost battalion. The guards were still guarding us, the roll was still being called each morning, the curfew was still in effect, and the meager rations were still being dipped out ladle by miserable ladle.

One morning an American plane zoomed low

153

over our compound. It was so close we could see the pilot, and every dormitory emptied as we rushed to the central quadrangle to wave and shout. He circled and zoomed over us again, this time waving and shouting something himself. After several passes someone got the idea that he was trying to signal us to clear the compound. No one would go inside—we didn't want to miss the excitement and were curious as to just what was coming next. We huddled together and flattened ourselves against the walls of buildings to watch.

Parachutes puffed out from his hatch, huge white billows from the sky dropping drums of provisions. I wanted to rush immediately and look at one, but was severely held back by the adults beside me.

Pass after pass was made as the manna from heaven crashed down to bounce and roll all over the compound, some indeed splintering through the roofs of our buildings, and some others landing outside our walls and onto the homes of the Chinese. Fortunately no one was killed or injured and reparations were later made for all damages.

When his cargo was totally unloaded, the pilot made one more pass and, together with the other members of his crew, signaled the V for victory sign and droned away into the horizon.

The Central Camp Committee had a massive task. The drums had to be gathered and emptied and the stores stacked for distribution. Everyone helped. British discipline would not tolerate a free-for-all grab (and believe me, I was ready to grab!) and we had to wait our turn in line.

Cans of fruit—peaches! We had not seen any fruit

154

whatsoever for two and a half years! Vitamin-enriched chocolate bars, one small square of which held a day's nutrition, or so the wrapper said! Powdered milk (Klim), tinned meat (Spam), and, of course, cartons and cartons of cigarettes. We all sat on our cots that night and feasted. We had been cautioned not to eat too much too soon, so we nibbled and snatched and savored. I doubt that anyone slept. Waves of laughter and excitement rippled through the dormitories as we sat on the threshold of release.

Later a draw was held among the girls for the many white parachutes that had floated our provisions down to earth. I was lucky enough to win one—an enormous nylon circle, astounding in texture. We had never seen anything like it.

"I'll save it and make my wedding dress from it," I thought, as it was rolled tight and given to me.

The American Army was on its way. Girls who had hoarded their lipsticks for this very occasion pulled them out. Fortunately we were not in the middle of a drought season: clothes were washed, hair and bodies were washed. It was one of the few times the showers in the bathhouse could be turned on with adequate water! Faces were prettied to greet the American soldiers.

They arrived within a day: our liberating task force of one lieutenant and two medics! They looked beautiful, tall and lanky in their khakis, but where were the others? The prettied faces and lipsticked mouths of the girls trembled in disappointment as they looked for the rest of an army that was not there.

The officer and his aides ate a couple of our meals

155

of SOS and almost immediately came down with severe cases of dysentery. We had to nurse them through most of a week! They were followed by the British task force, again disappointing—only three lonely officers. The combined task forces began to work with our Central Camp Committee to arrange for our transport back to Shanghai.

We did not see the Japanese guards or Yokomoto again. They had remained at their posts until the task forces arrived for the takeover, and during that time camp discipline had wisely kept our schedule the same. It would not have done to have hundreds of ill-nourished internees wandering around Yangchow, let loose on the city.

The officers decided we needed a celebration. They arranged with local Chinese officials to hire a band and prepare a feast. It was a celebration never to be forgotten. A small platform for the band was brought in. The camp ensemble was a conglomeration of Chinese drums, fiddles, flutes, and cymbals, trying their hardest to produce Americanized rhythms. What came out was a wailing banshee version of "Amapola" and "Frenesi" embellished by strains of "John Brown's Body," a Chinese funeral favorite!

Some of the internees tried dancing to the weird beat, and with the eerie moonlight casting shadows across the compound wall, and the gaunt figures trying to be festive, I felt I was being pushed, like Alice, through a looking-glass into a world of mystic fantasy.

The native pastors from local Yangchow Christian churches came in to make contact with the

156

missionaries and invited us to a service of thanksgiving. What a service it was! Some sixty or seventy of us went out from the camp to worship. Sermons were given in Chinese and translated by our missionaries into English; sermons were then given in English and translated into Chinese. We sang together:

We gather together to ask the Lord's blessing;
He chastens and hastens his will to make known.
The wicked oppressing now cease from distressing;
Sing praises to his name; He fails not his own!

Beside us to guide us, our God with us joining;
Ordaining, maintaining his kingdom divine.
So from the beginning the fight we were winning;
Lord, thine be all the glory; The victory is thine!

The Chinese sang in Chinese to their own tune and we sang in English to our own tune, and if anyone didn't know the tune, he just tried to blend in. The harmony would have made Bach turn over in his grave, but it was loud, cheerful, and sincere. I think Almighty God was very pleased, and I think the spirit of Hudson Taylor was very pleased!

The authorities decided that we would return to Shanghai overland via train, a day and a night's journey. Suddenly we were all faced with the moment of truth. Yangchow had been our cage; yet more, it was a security from the bombardments of war (we were relatively safe compared to those who had gone through the blitz in England), and for a brief period of time the pressures and demands of society had been lifted.

Through all the traumas of near-starvation, lack
of sanitation, and the thirsts of drought,
relationships had been welded together and a
camaraderie built among the internees. Of
necessity, attitudes had been modified and the basic
values of life reassessed.

On my last walk around the wall with Dobbs, I ran
my fingers along the rough brick, all the way
around the perimeter of the camp. I needed to touch
our confinement. Somehow I was almost sorry to
leave. We paused a moment by the clump of bushes
that was our Bible study classroom, where D. J. had
opened the Gospels to my confused heart and where
he had poured out his own heart in prayer for our
spiritual growth just the day before. Dobbs and I
paused another moment by the shadows where we
had so recently been in each other's arms—that
was our own private place. There was no privacy
now; it seemed the entire camp was pacing the wall
in one final walk. Were we ready to reenter the life
beyond it, and just what had happened to that life?

We packed and as I stashed Dog Toby into a
small suitcase that I was to carry personally, I gave
him a hug and said, "We made it, Toby, you and
I, we made it!" He was still stuffed full of money,
our security and aid to reentry.

Scrambling into trucks we made our way to the
railway station. We did not have to tote our
belongings this time, except for those of immediate
personal need. The task forces loaded baggage and
bedding to be sorted by the Red Cross at the other
end. The Bradley boys (no longer boys now, but
handsome young men) did not need their long

bamboo pole this time.

Chinese trains were not the most stable in the world! We were squashed in very tightly, which meant sitting up all night. An infection on my heel had swollen and was full of pus. I thought of Julie and my heart leaped at the possibility of seeing her again. I thought of my father. I had received four Red Cross letters from him and knew he was in Camp "N" Hong Kong.

The clickety-clack of the wheels sang "going-home, going-home," but where was "home," I wondered?

Narrow Escape

THE HUGE EMBANKMENT building apartment complex facing the Soochow Creek was chosen as Shanghai's central rehabilitation center for released POWs. Trains and trucks disgorged us there and quartered us in some two floors, where the excellent services of the International Red Cross helped join families and gather together the pieces of our broken lives. The other floors of the building were filled with American GIs, many of whom had just

Sampan villages on Soochow Creek.

returned from the Burma campaign and were
awaiting transportation to the States.

Bursting with the exhilaration of being back in
civilization after the devastation of the jungle, their
pockets laden with back pay, they were a roaring and
jubilant crowd. I was under strict instructions not to
fraternize with them, and under no circumstances
was I to venture up to the roof garden where so
many of them spent their leisure time.

The infection in my heel continued to give me
major problems, and as my mother had been
hospitalized after the rigors of our internment were
over, my aunt took me down to the medics who had
set up their clinic on the floor beneath our own
quarters. The cheers and wolf whistles that greeted
our swinging skirts as we walked through the
corridors inflated my feminine ego and I beamed
and waved at the men as I went for my shot of
penicillin.

Before long I was leaning over our balcony talking
to the GIs on their balconies on the various levels
beneath me and then, like Rapunzel who let down
her hair, I was told to let down a string onto which
they tied cans of candy and other goodies from the
American PX. I'd haul in my treasures and share
them with friends in adjacent quarters.
GI-watching became our favorite sport!

They flung nickels and dimes down to the
scampering Chinese coolies, gathered with arms
outstretched on the pavement beneath, and I had to
be restrained from dashing down to join the
hustling crowd on the street and pick up my own
share of the glittering silver coins. We were

desperately poor—everything had been lost in the war, and the currency in faithful old Dog Toby was practically worthless. We would have done better to have stuffed him with vitamin pills!

From time to time troupes of gaily dressed traveling Chinese acrobats would come and perform on the street beneath the balconies. As a crowd gathered around them, it became the sport of the GIs not only to throw their coins but to fill the condoms which they had been issued with water, tie the end, and then toss the makeshift balloons down to burst on the heads of the laughing Chinese. I had no idea what the balloons were or where they came from, but I decided that this was great sport and that the American soldiers were a lot of fun.

Julie and I were reunited in the embankment building. We flung our arms around each other, cried tears of joy, and then spent days and nights sitting cross-legged on my bed comparing the experiences of our imprisonment.

Her long pigtails had grown another foot, and now they trailed several inches beneath her hips. The blackness of her dark eyes accentuated her pale, thin face. As we were shortly to find out, Julie had tuberculosis.

Reinforced by a comrade-in-arms and mutually sustained by the memory of all our previous escapades, we decided to venture up onto the forbidden roof garden. It was a gorgeous, sunny autumn day and one could look down at the city of Shanghai and watch the pedicabs, trams, and bustling bodies streaming up and down the streets,

like the quick scurrying of colonies of ants.
Interspersed were the uniformed figures of the GIs
and American and British sailors, moving in groups
from the many ships that now crammed the
Whangpoo and were anchored along the Bund
waterfront.

We spent a delightful hour that afternoon chatting
and singing with many of the GIs. One had a dear
little monkey captured from the Burma jungle, and
he fascinated us with his tricks and comic antics.
Two of the soldiers suggested that we get together
again that evening, so we arranged to sneak out and
meet them on the roof garden at 7 P.M.

"I'll twist my hair around my head," said Julie. "It'll
make me look older. What are you going to wear?"

We pinched our cheeks and pushed through the
doors that opened onto the blinking heavens. The
nighttime scents wafted up from the sampan
village on the Soochow Creek. They were there,
the men in khaki, smoking cigarettes, waiting for us.
We chewed gum and chatted and laughed with them
awhile, and then Julie sauntered off with her GI to
look at the view from the other side of the roof.

My GI took a long draw on his cigarette, flicked it
over the roof, and then put his arm around my
waist. I smiled up at him, and before I realized what
he was up to, he had pushed me flat down on my
back and pinioned me on the wide ledge atop the
small wall that served as a guardrail of the roof
garden.

His mouth clamped roughly on mine so that I
could not scream, and he started unzipping his
pants and pulling down my skirt. I knew that if I

164

budged an inch I could roll both of us off the ledge to drop four or five stories down and smash onto the concrete street below. Just a few days before, someone had jumped out of one of the windows and we had all looked out from our balconies to see his blood-spattered body being covered with a sheet by the U. S. medics who had rushed to the scene.

Vividly I imagined my own blood-spattered body on the pavement below with blood trickling out of my mouth and ears! The weight of his chest and shoulders crushed the breath out of me and the military brass buttons on his jacket dug into the tenderness of my chest.

Rape is the terror of any woman under captivity. How ironic that my own encounter came, not with an enemy soldier, but with one of our own, an American GI!

"O God," I prayed, "O God, help me, help me!"

Within moments Julie's giggling chatter came around the corner.

"Hey, Fay, let's go, they're going to start missing us downstairs."

She was walking back toward us, arm in arm with her GI. Cursing violently, my GI got off me, zipped up his pants, and walked quickly to the stairway. My trembling hands rearranged my skirt and blouse. I was shaking. I was mortified at my stupidity. I was very frightened. I was crying.

Thank God for the darkness that covered my twisted face. Thank God for hearing my prayer. Thank God for protecting me and delivering me from my own folly.

Angel of God, my guardian dear,
To whom his love commits me here,
Ever this day be at my side,
To light and guard, to rule and guide.

"Thank you, my guardian angel," I whispered the prayer over and over.

With the inside of my lips bleeding from where they had been crushed against my teeth, and with my heart numb with shame, I went to bed and sobbed myself to sleep.

I never went to the roof garden again.

Letters from D. J.

REPATRIATION was uppermost in everyone's mind.
Families which had been separated through the war
yearned to unite and reestablish themselves "back
home"—in England, Australia, Europe, Canada, or
the United States. They faced malnutrition, broken
bodies, broken spirits, devastated finances (the
Chinese dollar was practically worthless and it was
necessary to carry around suitcases of currency in
order to pay for even the simplest of services such as a

167

rickshaw ride). A general apprehension of the future sent people scurrying to cram into every available vessel in a swarming exodus out of Shanghai. It became a text of manipulative skill to see who could wangle a passage on the first repatriation ship.

Businessmen anchored to the Far Eastern trade sent their wives and children on ahead while they regrouped and restaffed. Missionaries who had committed their entire lives to spreading the love of Jesus Christ throughout China sought permission from their various societies to visit their mission stations before the long trek home. D. J. Watson put his family on the repatriation ship *Araw* bound for London, and then went back to the Leper Hospital in Hankow.

Through all the traumas of rebuilding the faith in the local Chinese community, he maintained total communication with those of us in his Yangchow Bible study classes. "My little children, of whom I travail in birth again until Christ be formed in you..." (Galatians 4:19). We were his children in the Lord, his responsibility to nourish in spiritual growth. For the next eleven years his letters arrived to exhort, instruct, admonish, or commend me in the faith. They stopped only after my marriage, when he handed over the reins of spiritual leadership to my husband.

Hankow, China
November 1945

My dear Fay,
   It is nearly three weeks since we had a conversation, and naturally I am wondering whether you and your

mother have managed to secure a flat in some quiet area where your mother will not feel unduly bothered.

After the repatriation ship Araw sailed, I saw in the Shanghai newspaper that she might travel via Australia. Both Steve and I hoped not, for it would have lengthened the voyage appreciably, and that would have been no joke for our families down in those airless 'tween decks. However, I received a wireless message from Alice at Singapore the other day, to my great surprise and pleasure (for I had not dreamed of such a possibility), saying that they had been allowed up to a higher deck along with other friends, and everything was going well. This has been a great relief, and as Alice does not mention Australia, we imagine that the vessel is going direct to London and will arrive there before Christmas. By the way, I had hoped to be back in Shanghai by then, but I fear that we shall have to spend it here as there is so much to do.

Steve and I were welcomed back to this center during service in the Griffith John Memorial Church last Sunday. We were referred to as the exiles who have returned to Jerusalem after slavery in Babylon! Not a bad comparison, even if I had not grown a square-cut Babylonian beard during the ensuing years!

I have been taken for various types of people in China; a man was puzzled over my khaki shorts and rucksack. He wondered if I was a Russian officer or an Armenian carpet-seller. On the voyage up river a Danish scientist wasn't sure whether I was a GI or a Roman Catholic priest! Now, however, I must look like the prophet Ezekiel returning from Babylon. I always pictured Ezekiel as a long, thin, miserable-looking fellow, so perhaps I resemble him!

169

Keep up your spirits; work hard (need I say that?);
be always considerate of your mother; look ahead to that
school abroad to which you are going and maintain your
daily devotions, remembering ever that prayer I copied
for you shortly before leaving Yangchow.

Blessings on you, lassie,
D. J. Watson

Hankow, China
December 1945

My dear Fay,

It was good to receive your letter and the news of your
father having made that splendid offer for your
schooling in Switzerland. I can only see one possible
snag, and that is that your mother, having (as she often
says) been disillusioned so many times, may argue that the
letter is mere words and cannot possibly come true. I
wonder. However, she has said that it is time that your
father undertook the responsibility of your education, so
maybe she will let you go.

What a welcome you will get! He'll fairly spoil you if
I know anything about it. Mind you, brush your hair as I
like it; none of those ringlets, and then, perhaps, you'll
please him! Just be natural.

Poor old Dobbs will be brokenhearted when you
leave. I shall have to console him with a stiff history essay
to do—just to take his mind off things, lest the unhappy
youth throws himself in that muddy and unromantic
ditch called Soochow Creek!

I feel sorry for these GIs who come in from the country
and stay in Shanghai for a while before sailing. You must
remember that most of these boys have not seen a
European girl for years, so that when they meet people

170

like you and Julie they fall (or think they are falling) in love. By the time these youths have been home in the States a few months they will settle down into normal citizens. Be nice to them, but no more. Above all, don't throw kisses away—it can be dangerous, especially with these fellows. Kisses arouse them so that they want more and more of you, and you might find yourself in a difficult situation if you are not careful. I pray for my lassie every day.

Steve and I have returned from a visit to Siaokan, my former station up country. The welcome was rather overwhelming from Christians and non-Christians alike, and everybody wanted to know when we were going to reopen the hospital. The buildings proper have not suffered as badly as we thought, but everything has been looted. You may remember me telling you that I had left my best books, certificates, important papers, and my camera in boxes in the leper hospital. Alas! Everything has gone. I must not moan when so many people have lost homes and loved ones, but I had scraped ever since my student days to build up those treasures; some of them were college prizes. Never mind. One must learn "in whatsoever state one is, therein to be content..." as Saint Paul says.

The lepers have suffered terribly; of sixty-six brethren in the colony when I left in '42 there are only nineteen left alive. They lacked food, medicines, and clothes, poor fellows. I was able to take them some aid contributed locally, and they were grateful. Today I have sent a strong report to London (Mission to Lepers) requesting aid to be sent out at once.

There is much for us to do here; heartening the leaders, preparing for a forward movement in the near future, settling problems here and there. We are on the go the whole time. It is satisfactory to know that our visit is so necessary. Actually, I am typing this to you late at night. Hankow possesses neither light nor heat. It is cold; I must turn in soon. My candle is nearly out.

Yours very sincerely,
D. J. Watson

Hankow, China
December 1945

My dear Fay,

At the risk of our letters crossing again I feel that I must write to you in reply to your letter which only reached me the day before yesterday. I pictured a woeful lassie trying to be very brave, but with her hopes and dreams fading away.

We must face realities; you cannot depend upon anything reliable coming from your father. I do not doubt that he is full of good intentions and that he is longing for his daughter, but I can't see anything being based on his promises. I feel so sorry for him.

Now before that bolt came out of the blue, promising you an education in Switzerland, your hope was for your mother to get a furlough shortly and for you to go with her to England or Canada, or even to Australia. We must go back to that hope and pray for it to be accomplished. Your mother remembers her own education in Shanghai, and she is a remarkable woman. But we have to face the fact that Shanghai is not what it was and is rapidly becoming less and less a center in which young ladies can gain the right culture and attitude to life if they are to become good citizens and able to pull their weight in a Christian home.

172

By now you will have received my last letter in which I announced the fact that I cannot reach Shanghai before the end of January or beginning of February. Thus you have plenty of time in which to write me fairly often. Write me just as you feel and as often as you like. I can stand it all—whether you blow off, feel sad, affectionate, or angry. But again let me say, for goodness' sake, don't call me "sir"!

I will possibly annoy you by ending with some spelling corrections, but I must risk that if I am to be the help that I want to be; you must be able to write essays without losing marks unnecessarily. "Merry Christmas" needs capitals, as I have given them. "Especially" not "espically"; "length" not "lenght"; "opportune" not "oppotune"; "officialdom" has no "e" on the end; "delivered" not "dilivered." Don't let these few remarks discourage you, so that you say, "I'd better not write if my letters are full of mistakes like that"; no, the more you write the more I can correct, so that later people will say, "How well she expresses herself!"

Don't feel down over anything I write; do believe that I am trying to be helpful. Be kind to good old Dobbs, who sends me the most wonderful epistles these days, full of Christian grace and expressiveness. That fellow will turn out a missionary one of these days (don't tell him) and when I am old I shall meet him in China, possibly working in some unorthodox but helpful way and being an uplift wherever he goes.

"Maintain the spiritual glow..." Remember, Romans 8:28 is still true, whether one translates it in the King James Version, "And we know that all things work together for good to them that love God, to them who are the called according to his purpose..." or direct from

173

the Greek into modern English: "*Those who love God,
those who have been called in terms of his purpose, have
his aid and interest in everything.*"

Blessings on you, dear lassie; I pray constantly that
you may be upheld and strengthened.

Yours sincerely,
D. J. Watson

On board H. M. Transport
"The Highland Chieftan"
February 1946

My dear Fay,

So sorry to learn from Dobbs that you are laid up
again with a bout of bronchitis. I had hoped to see you
again before leaving Shanghai. Dobbs and I had a
splendid talk together on Thursday morning and
wouldn't you like to know what we said about you!

Now we are running S. to S. W. 'round the coast,
expecting to reach H. Kong in about three days.
Conditions on board are much better for women and
children than they were on Araw—bunks for everyone,
and they eat in the dining saloon. We men (except those
over 55) are terribly squashed up down in the lower
'tween decks, and we sleep (or try to) in hammocks
which are so close that we bump one another the whole
time. I'm not grumbling. Great fun for those of us with a
sense of humor. Folks are mixed: under the hammocks
are two Frenchmen, two Danes, a R. C. priest (Irish),
two Scotsmen, and the rest of us nondescript
Englishmen. I shall survive–smiling!

Blessings on you, dear lassie, is my constant prayer.

Yours very sincerely,
D. J. Watson

My very dear Fay,

Two letters of yours to answer—something new! I am
grateful for both of them, especially the one telling me
of how someone was walking on air at the very idea of
getting away from Shanghai to Canada. These letters are
really very good, Fay, and show what you can do when
you have time and feel like expressing yourself—even to
letting out to your Father Confessor that you really like
dear old Dobbs quite a lot!

I think of you and pray for you every day—generally
the last thing at night or first thing in the morning, but
sometimes at odd times on the tops of buses and in all
sorts of odd places. That you may be blessed of God,
that he will build you up in soul and character and
grant you the best in happiness and insight into
life, and that the result may be usefulness, quietness,
and peace. In some ways I feel that the prayer is
already being answered, but it is a life process and I
shall, of course, go on praying. Do you pray for Dobbs?
OF COURSE!! It is easy to pray for some people. Well,
remember me too, for I have so much to do and to
prepare, and I feel sorely lacking oftimes in wisdom and
power.

Alice and I have a home of our own again at last.
We are in the top flat of one of the houses belonging to
our Society, and it is in such pretty surroundings—we get
fine views all 'round of hills and woodland.

The ruined castle of Earl Warrenne, Earl of Surrey,
who lost the Battle of Stirling Bridge against Wallace in
1296, lies a mile to the west. Mark and Alice and I
explored the ruins last Friday and enjoyed the beautiful

175

rose garden where once stood the banqueting hall.

The settling in has been a busy time for us. I spent a lot of time on my knees (how pious, said she!). Ha! Cutting old linoleum to shape! Humping furniture around is no joke either.

Sometimes, you know, I get worried about you. It's not that I fear you will become an atheist or backslide, just a fearful gloom that you may start to let second-rate things take first place in your life. It's not that movies or dances are bad in themselves, they need not be, and you know that I am anything but a killjoy. But one has to see to it that they do not take first place in one's interest or lead on to other things.

I understand very well how you feel in longing to belong intensely to someone and in wanting loving kisses to be showered upon you. On these occasions you would do well to read something interesting or do something that will take your mind off the longing until it passes. Someday—please God—a good fellow will come along and you will fall mutually in love (Dobbs seems to think he's that fellow!). But keep a firm grip over yourself until marriage is an accomplished thing. Then you will both feel that you want to give and give intensely to one another, and your joy will be full—in giving and in receiving.

How I wish that we could talk over some of these things—letters are poor substitutes. I want the thoughts of the Master himself to become your thoughts, and for you to become the splendid Christian woman you can be. I think so often of the day you knelt before me in camp and I placed my hand on your head and received you into the church. You are my daughter in the Lord and I love you dearly.

Blessings to you and your mother.

Yours sincerely,
D. J. Watson

Surrey, England
June 1946

My dear Fay,

Although I wrote last time (for your birthday) you are due a reply to the long and excellent letter which crossed mine. Yes, you are improving in your expressions and in the use of English.

Now to your questions about God. It is a pity that most people do not bother to ask themselves these same questions. The fact that you have struck such a rock is no shame. This, Fay dear, will actually prove to be another stepping stone upward. Difficulties work out that way, but because I want to help you I am sending this by return mail so that you won't have long to wait.

Think of God as the almighty power and purpose behind the universe. How do we know God? In nature, in science, in our consciences, but chiefly by the remarkable way in which Hebrew prophetic minds, one after another and in ever rising succession, found God to be holy, perfect, personal, and merciful in dealing with men and women and nations. The complete revelation of course came in Jesus of Nazareth.

Think of Jesus first of all as a human teacher who knew hunger and want, disappointment and happiness, and who prayed in agony as we sometimes do. Yet, because of his indwelling divine Spirit, the power and purpose of God dominated his heart and will, and in these things he was completely at one with God. He was God manifest in human form (read Philippians 2:5-11).

177

That is why when we think of God (whom we have not seen) we think of him in terms of Jesus (who, through the Scriptures, we have seen).

Jesus said, "When you pray say, 'Father...'" So, unlike you, I address all my prayers to God as Father, but my praying is based upon what I know of Jesus. That is why most people conclude their prayers with phrases such as "through Jesus Christ our Lord," or "in the name of Jesus." These mean, "This prayer to thee is based on Jesus, and is offered in (what I hope is) the spirit of Jesus–the way in which he prayed." We end our prayers with the simple word "Amen," the Hebrew word which means "So let it be!"

Now where do human beings come in? We are unlike the rest of creation in that the Almighty has given us the power of moral choice. Limited we are, by heredity, environment, and a host of other things, but we can, within these limits, make decisions. Why is this? There can be only one answer. God wants to win us into sonship and daughterhood, and therefore he has deliberately limited himself, and taken the terrific risk of losing us, so that we may decide freely for ourselves. A dog or machine can make no moral or spiritual response, but we can.

We see God's love for us written large in creation and in the love of friends, but chiefly we see it poured out for us in Jesus Christ (i.e., the Messiah–the Anointed One), who suffered unjustly upon the cross–killed by what were considered to be the "best" people of that age. The cross shows up the bankruptcy of human nature without the gospel.

Shall we refuse that appeal which God makes to us? We are free to live selfishly if we choose, and so cause unrest and trouble and war. Or shall we make a response and say, "Lord, I too would join thy family as an active member. Take me, with all my faults and shortcomings, just as I am; and think through my mind, and speak through my lips, and set my heart on fire for thy cause"?

Is this any more clear to you now? I wish we could pore over the Scriptures together as we did in camp and I could see your eyes light up and hear you say, "Ah yes, now I see it!"

Down from the sublime and on to your dancing.... Some people believe it is of the devil, but on the whole you'll find missionaries to have broader views (odd as it may seem) than some other folk, so they ask "What kind of dancing is it, and before what kind of people is it being performed?" It is narrow-minded people who lump all dancing together as equal when it obviously isn't. Scottish highland dancing performed to the wail of bagpipes is delightful, and some of the folk dances of Europe are charming. Most of us are interested in the art and grace of the dancing, but you must realize that there are certain youths who only go to see as much as they can of a girl's legs.

Now I'm going to be very frank with you, my dear lassie, and I hope that you won't be hurt, but when you danced in camp, did you consider your audience? Most of the people present enjoyed your dancing, but certain youths were obviously present for a different reason. If you could have heard the remarks in the meal queue the following morning, you would have blushed furiously. Lads like that see a girl partly undressed, say in a south sea grass skirt, and that makes them long for more. They go to bed that night thinking lascivious things about her. I know youths and so I know what I am talking about.

This was proved by the remarks which I overheard in the queue the following day, and which caused me to feel very angry with the young men in question and want to crack their heads together.

It is good to know about the things that are in your heart and that are puzzling you. I only hope that my remarks above have not hurt you in any way; they are not meant to do so.

Perhaps your next letter will be from Vancouver! I think it's about time you gave up addressing me stiffly as "Mr. Watson." Most of the young people whom I taught and counseled in camp call me D. J. That's fine unless you would like to come up with some special title of your own!

Blessings on you, my dear lassie. I pray for you daily.

Yours sincerely,
D. J. Watson

Ashiway, Ah-nee'! (Good-bye, Ah-nee'!)

"SOUNDS MARVELOUS, but how much key money?"

Black market housing was thriving. Housing had always been a problem in overcrowded Shanghai, but the postwar city was teeming not only with released POWs awaiting repatriation or rehabilitation, but with personnel from all the allied Far Eastern forces for whom billets had to be found. It was the custom for landlords and/or former tenants

181

to demand "key money"—a set sum for even a reference to a vacancy.

The Japanese occupation forces had commandeered houses, flats, furniture, and anything that took their fancy. Even Pickles, the monkey belonging to the people with whom we shared a house just prior to our incarceration, had been "tagged" by the group of Japanese officers. They came through stamping their paper seals on all the items they wanted to have left intact for their use.

They stared, pointed, and giggled at Pickles in his huge wire cage on the enclosed veranda, and Pickles in return bared his teeth, rattled the wire, and chattered back at them. We were pleased to let them have anything they wanted, as all of us had gone ashen white at the thought that perhaps they had come to drag the elderly father, Mr. G., off to Bridge House!

The whole world had gone cockeyed! Bank accounts were valueless, possessions had been devastated, and everyone was struggling to put together a puzzle from which just too many pieces of their lives were missing.

Hong Kong was making a brisk recovery, as described in these excerpts from an article written by my father and published in the Adelaide *Advertiser* in the spring of 1946:

A few months ago, silent and sad-eyed, they lined the fence of the prison camp, begging for food. Now ... the children smile and sing again in Hong Kong!

They seem to have suddenly blossomed like, say peonies, because they were not on the streets before.

182

They will not hesitate to flag a jeep and get a lift when they are late, and they will reach for the hand of any Commando or sailor who passes.

What more cogent comment can I offer on Hong Kong's recovery? Let me step the tempo up by saying that I saw a child of about six bowled over by a jeep a few weeks ago. He was gathered up into a hospital, thoroughly built up so that he was plump and strong, rigged in Marine Commando's kit from gaiters to beret, and swaggers now like any sergeant.

Yet during our internment, emaciated children, with swollen legs and bones bursting through thigh and cheek, lined the fence of our prison camp, silent and lethargic. From our meager rations of rice each day we were still able to feed them.

The Navy came in here to find hospitals denuded and filthy. One ship, HMS Artifex, took on the job of reequipment; and now Queen Mary Hospital is run like a warship with loudspeakers calling technical staff, with an almost automatic X-ray service, and, what is the most convincing, a beaming bevy of Chinese girls who learn what nursing service means from our own St. John's Nursing Order.

But there is a more sinister side. Crime is prevalent in the form of armed robbery. In recent judgments the magistrate has ordered caning as well as imprisonment, and Commandos will not hesitate to open fire at night when men challenged do not stop.

The process of cleansing the Colony has taken time, for, in the apathy of their realization of defeat, the Japanese left the place in a filthy condition. Now they themselves are employed in the cleansing!

The harbor is full of ships of the British Pacific Fleet,

ASHIWAY, AH-NEE!

with the Duke of York *as the flagship, which flies Admiral Lord Fraser's flag. The streets are full of sailors and soldiers. The curio dealers reap a rich harvest. The black market has been broken by government action* which should be an example to Shanghai.

As I write, the roar of 10,000 people from the football field surges into my flat. "Services v. Combined China"–the admiral and governor are there and so is a general. In this Colony there is now justice and fair play. Administration has been magnificent, recovery lively and brisk.

Without colonial governmental action, Shanghai was not doing as well. Far from being "broken," the black market continued to thrive.

My mother was making a slow recovery in the hospital. Her spirits were bolstered one day by the visit of a friend who offered to let her take over his duplex flat with, miracle of miracles, no key money! He was going home on leave and hoped eventually to return. It was a generous, splendid gesture and we snapped it up.

Situated in a court of similar apartments on *Rue Boissezon* in the French Concession (if indeed there were any concessions left!) it was a two-bedroom, comfortably furnished lower duplex, complete with a small garden and servants' quarters over the garage. Two bachelors occupied the upper duplex and roared their way through party after party, fraternizing with the RAF officers billeted nearby. They were cheerful, fascinating neighbors.

With the duplex, we had inherited a resident "boy"

184

who was an adequate cook, and we shared the services of a coolie who came in regularly to clean and dust. The social swim had resumed, intensified by the presence of the fleet, which meant dinners in ward rooms and a constant round of parties. Shanghai was never normal, but life was beginning to take on somewhat of a prewar exuberant flavor. I was coming of age and so was included in all the activities that my mother felt would enhance my manners and social graces. Dinners on battleships thrilled me the most, when the port was passed around, ending the evening with toasts to the King!

Shortages were everywhere—it was practically impossible to get fuel of any kind, and I remember one particularly cold evening when my mother in desperation ordered the boy to break up a chair for a fire. Hot water was still a luxury. We'd have it hauled in from the street "water sellers" and I'd take a bath in mother's water, or vice versa. Our duplex had a modern, regular bath tub, which I felt was a pity. One of the B & S houses we had lived in had a lovely huge ceramic Chinese kong tub, with a little seat in it. This had meant sitting up to the neck in piping hot water, a glorious feeling!

The American PX had probably the only supply of nylon stockings around, and the black market hawkers did a thriving business in them. Despite all the shortages, the champagne still flowed—we had survived!

A lot of people hadn't. Articles appeared in the *North China Daily News* carrying reports of atrocities and strangely, quite a few people suddenly seemed

185

to drop dead in their tracks. Heart attacks on the streets, or in places of business, or at the clubs … it was as though their energies, goaded by the fight to "make it through" internment, suddenly snapped in the relaxation of release.

The human body is tremendously resilient; it did not take us long to get "built up" a bit and functional. However, the human spirit had been severely tested and was to bear the lifetime scars of those tests, positive or negative. We were a people who would never be quite the same again.

Spiritually, I was uncomfortable. The traumas and reassessment of all my values in the years of internment could not be swept aside by the glitter and pomp of social traditions, much as I enjoyed them. The faith that D. J. had so carefully planted in my life gnawed at me, hungering and thirsting and demanding to be fed. I was restless and constantly yearning to dig out deeper meanings and purposes in life … and death. I yearned for more, and more, and still more of the knowledge of God. To know "… the breadth, and length, and depth, and height … the love of Christ, which passeth knowledge … filled with all the fulness of God …" (Ephesians 3:18, 19).

Across many waters, over many bridges, and through another lifetime of circumstances, some of that fullness was to come. And it will reach the totality of its fulfillment when at last I am folded against the bosom of the Father.

Through that crumbling, artificial world, letters from D. J. were my stability and guideline, anchored by the continuing contact with Dobbs.

Hastily the British School had been organized, taking over the facilities of the famous Cathedral School for Girls, and it was coeducational. Dobbs was there and so was I—at least for the few months it took to obtain our passages out of Shanghai. Just to feel his steady blue eyes on me gave me strength and drew me back from the frivolities of the social whirl to the foundations of "seek ye first the kingdom of God, and his righteousness...." I knew that my identity was with God and not in the circumstances around me. One might say that I had begun to walk in immortality.

This was tested one day when Keith arrived at our duplex door with a huge white basket of carnations. He had flagged my mother down while she was riding a rickshaw, delighted to find us again, and made the appointment to come and call. He was even more dashing, and handsome, and charming than I had remembered. But as we talked, and laughed, and flirted a bit, I knew that our time together was past. Never again would I be swayed by his world. I belonged to a different destiny, a destiny that I gripped in a little black book inscribed:

To Fay, with love, Carol.
Thy Word is a lamp unto my feet,
  and a light unto my path.

It was a destiny that said "Come unto me, all ye that labour and are heavy laden, and I will give you rest. Take my yoke upon you, and learn of me; for I am meek and lowly in heart: and ye shall find rest

187

unto your souls. For my yoke is easy, and my burden is light" (Matthew 11:28-30).

I looked at the laboring, heavy-laden Chinese. Their sorrows had been grafted into my childhood. They were part of the environment, to be accepted without question. Their men pulled my rickshaw, their women braided my hair, many of their children lived and died on the broad windowsills of the large European Banking Houses, and their personal tragedies grew like glaucoma over the eyes of my inner being.

Suddenly I saw them in the "Come unto me, all ye that labour and are heavy laden...." I saw them in the letters from D. J., I saw them in my own C.I.M. roots. Suddenly I identified with them. Suddenly I loved them.

I did not belong with the grandiose, the chiffons and finery, I belonged with the poor, the suffering, the uncared for. I looked at my hands and said, "Take them, Father; dirty them if you want to; use them!" Hands will wash, bodies will wash—it's hearts that are so difficult to cleanse.

Julie had tuberculosis. She was hospitalized and miserable. Her father was arranging passage home to Italy and trying to tie up his many business affairs at the same time. At last my mother had obtained passages for us to Canada and it was time for good-byes. Julie's beautiful dark eyes seemed to have sunk far into her golden skin, but the long braids wrapped around and around her head still shimmered in the sunlight of the hospital garden. I couldn't even kiss her for fear of contamination.

"I'll love you always."

"I'll love you, too."

"We'll write, always—all our life."

"Always."

She was later to write from her chaise lounge high in the Italian Alps where she was taking the "cure":

I am beginning to find life's true values and to live them with the result that one comes to distinguish between superfluities and that which is truly worthwhile. Whatever leads us to a fuller realization of our own personality (as human beings raised to the dignity of Temples of the Holy Ghost, each with an individual character and mission in God's plan of creation), and to our more intimate and personal union with our Lord, is worthwhile.

From my experiences I now fully realize that suffering has only one reason to be: to make one feel the utter inadequacy and helplessness of ourselves and all creatures and that our Creator and Father is our ALL. He will give us comfort in our moments of weakness (and physical weakness always affects one morally and spiritually) and strength almost to love our suffering because it gradually separates us and elevates us above the healthy fellow creatures around us who cannot understand us, who soon tire of us and our constant need of care. While we are slowly purified we lose our attachments to those around us in a constant ascent toward our Father, on whom our suffering eyes are fixed.

Dobbs gave me a pretty blue stone ring. He was going to his sister in California and then probably to Vancouver, my own destination. We knew we'd see

189

each other again.

"I love you," he said simply, as we clung to each other.

"Yes," I whispered, and then in a burst of sobs, "Oh, Dobbs, do pray for me; what will I ever do without you and D. J.?"

He dried my tears, and then, with the eyes of a counselor more than a young man in love, said sternly, "Jesus—he loves you more than anyone ever could. Remember, he will never leave you. He will never forsake you!"

A truck took our huge metal steamer trunks to the freighter, and my mother and I followed in a pedicab. Yes, the rickshaw was now being pulled by a bicycle and had room for two passengers. A great improvement not only to the riders, but to the dignity of the coolie.

We circled the famous racecourse and for a moment I heard once again the marching bands of British Colonial splendor. I saw the drum majors in their leopard skins, twirling their drumsticks; the High-landers with their swinging kilts and gleaming white helmets; the pipes playing "Cock of the North"; the turbanned sikhs riding huge horses as part of the police force display. The pageantry and uniformed glitter of the British Empire! I thought of my small brother in his cub scout uniform, who once, at such an occasion, handed out programs, his eyes growing wide with wonder as the Tommies threw together a suspension bridge in less than an hour.

Little did we know that a rebel called Mao Tse-tung was rallying his armies through the hills and countryside, and training his guerrilla fighters to

190

chase the Foreign Devils out of China. Behind us, the bamboo curtain was slowly starting to fall.

In the "Garden of Peaceful Brightness" in the park of the Jade Fountain, not far from the Summer Palace in Peking, stands a seven-story white marble pagoda. It was built by the Emperor Kang Hsi, a contemporary of Louis XIV, and is one of some 10,000 pagodas reputed to have existed in and around the Peiping countryside—beacons of the Chinese faith, the Chinese way. The pagoda was symbolic of a culture and a civilization with roots some 2,000 years before Christ. It held its people captive and bound in superstition that ground them into poverty and hunger. It was an era that was soon to explode into smitherines, to exist no more. We were stepping out of its final page in history.

I searched every face for Ah-Nee. She was not there. Bubbling Well Road, Nanking Road, our trips for the long needles of the Pasteur treatment; our visits to Jessfield Park; our treats at the tuck shop. Somewhere in the melee—where was she?

Coolies vied with each other to carry our heavy trunks on board ship. The Whangpoo was alive with every type of vessel imaginable. Statistics said that the Shanghai harbor could hold as many as 146 merchant vessels and twenty-two warships at once, besides all the miscellaneous small launches, junks, flat-bottom river boats, and sampans, as far as the eye could see.

Scavenger sampans mulled around the large ships with nets to catch their garbage and sift it through in the hopes of finding more supplements to their meager diets.

The whistle blew, and blew again. Slowly ropes
were set adrift and the ship pulled away from the
dock. There were no streamers thrown from the deck
to attach long lingering cords to the well-wishers
on the dock! I remembered past departures of
pleasure cruisers with webs of paper ribbons from all
three decks intertwined so thickly to those on the
docks that they formed a solid mass across the water.
Finally the ship would slip beyond the length of the
streamer and, almost on a given beat, they would all
snap and fall into the murky water.

There were no streamers now to bid us good-bye.
We were fortunate in getting a passage on a freighter
at all, and had to share a small cabin with two other
ladies bound for the New World.

I stood at the stern of the ship and watched the
propeller churn the muddy waters of the Whangpoo
into an ever-widening wake. The waterfront drifted
away and I looked up ... cloud formations had strung
themselves together to take the shape of a celestial
city, and I caught a brief vision of immortality.

Before I turned to face the new horizon, I pressed
my fingers to my lips, "*Ashiway*, Ah-Nee," I
whispered, "*Ashiway....*"